DESTINED FOR GLORY

Fulfilling God's Purpose
& Plan For Your Life

Bobby Hilton

TAKING THE WORD TO THE WORLD™

Unless otherwise indicated, all Scripture quotations are from the *King James Version* of the Bible.

Scripture quotations noted (*AMP*) are from *The Amplified Bible,* Expanded Edition, © 1987 by the Zondervan Corporation and the Lockman Foundation. Used by permission. All rights reserved.

Scripture quotations noted (*TLB*) are from *The Living Bible,* © 1971 by Tyndale House Publishers. Used by permission. All rights reserved.

Scripture quotations noted (*NIV*) are from the *Holy Bible, New International Version,* © 1973, 1978, and 1984 by the International Bible Society. Used by permission. All rights reserved.

Editorial note: We have chosen not to capitalize the name satan and related names. Emphasis within Scripture is the author's own.

ISBN 1-930766-28-9

Library of Congress Catalog Card Number 2002108924

Bishop Bobby Hilton Ministries, Inc.
690 Northland Blvd.
Forest Park, OH 45240
(513) 851-WORD (9673) • Fax: (513) 742-3458
Website: www.bobbyhilton.org

Dedication

Blessed be the God and Father of our Lord Jesus Christ,
who hath blessed us with all spiritual blessings
in heavenly places in Christ:

According as he hath chosen us in him
before the foundation of the world, that we should
be holy and without blame before him in love:

Having predestinated us unto the adoption
of children by Jesus Christ to himself,
according to the good pleasure of his will,

To the praise of the glory of his grace,
wherein he hath made us accepted in the beloved.
(Ephesians 1:3–6)

To God be all glory, honor, and praise for allowing me the opportunity to disseminate the information contained in this book.

I dedicate this book to all who are part of my destiny, especially:

My wife, Valda, my son, Jermaine, and my daughter, Stephanie; we are on this road together! I love you all very much.

June Ridgway and all who assisted in bringing this work to fruition; your labor is so very much appreciated.

The family of "The Word;" thank you for your continued prayers and support.

Bishop Andrew and Pastor Viveca Merritt; I could not ask the Lord for a greater spiritual covering. Thank you so much!

Everyone who supports this ministry; I thank God for ordaining you—at this time—to assist in what He has destined for my life.

Table of Contents

Preface

On our path to destiny, there may be obstacles and difficulties, which discourage and disrupt us. However, believers must understand that we are not here by accident, coincidence, or mistake. God knows the challenges each of us will face before we are conceived in our mothers' wombs. In His omniscience, He has provided us with the breakthroughs and miracles that enable us to make it through. This is why we must never forget that God is sovereign and holds all power. He alone determines that no matter what comes against us, we will fulfill His purpose, and our lives will glorify Him.

In this book, my assignment is to remind and encourage the body of Christ that we are created for His glory (Isaiah 43:7). We were established as God's centerpiece and main attraction before the world began. Of all His wonderful creations—Heaven, earth, sun, moon, and stars—God chooses to place His crown of glory and honor upon man (Psalm 8:5). As we remain submitted to God, His purpose shall be manifested through our lives.

Paul informs us—in Romans 8:18—of the attitude he had towards life's challenges: "For I reckon that the sufferings of this present time are not worthy to be compared with the glory which shall be revealed in us." We must keep our spirits filled with God's Word, and remain confident that regardless of how difficult situations become, the glorious life God intended shall come to pass.

Our road of destiny includes many "predetermined moments" that God has declared for us. These moments are designed to give Him glory. As we approach these milestones of life, it may seem that things are bleak, dark, miserable, and even desolate. This is the time we must operate by faith and not by sight, knowing that the radiance of God's glory will soon appear.

I pray that this book will bring encouragement and strength to you. Do not allow the trials of this life to diminish your trust and confidence that you are *Destined for Glory. God's purpose and plan shall be fulfilled in your life!*

Bishop Bobby Hilton, Ph.D.

Introduction

Is there a reason for our existence? What is God's plan for mankind? Why are we here and what is our destiny? Most people who are honest with themselves will acknowledge—at some point in their lives—that they have asked these or similar questions. In the chapters that follow, my goal is to provide biblically framed answers for understanding God's purpose and plan for our lives. We will explore how Christians, as the body of Christ, are destined to be an expression of God's glory on the earth. Ultimately, in fulfillment of God's eternal purpose, we shall be glorified with our Lord and Savior (Romans 8:17, 30); and as glorified believers, we will be one with Christ.

Chapter one begins with an analysis of the intimate relationship Adam and Eve enjoyed with the Creator before their fall in the Garden of Eden. It examines their spiritual disconnection from God, and how this led to mankind's proclivity to distraction and loss of focus on our true purpose. Believers cannot afford to be naïve about the enemy's tricks. In this chapter, satan's strategy to compromise God's purpose and plan for mankind is systematically uncovered.

Chapter two explores the concept of predestination. It explains how believers were ordained as children of the Father, through Jesus Christ, before the foundation of the world (Ephesians 1:4). Before time began, we were *saved* and *called* with a holy calling for His purpose and glory (2 Timothy 1:9). This chapter provides assurance that no matter how things look, God's counsel (decree) shall stand (Isaiah 46:10) and our destiny shall come to pass (Psalm 37:5).

Chapter three provides an in-depth examination of *God's answer* to the dilemma caused by Adam and Eve's disobedience. Included is a theological exegesis of God's declaration, "Let there be light" (Genesis 1:3). Many Christians mistakenly believe that the light referred to in this Scripture is describing the creation of the sun and moon. This chapter offers a different view. It posits that Jesus is revealed as the Light that was called forth to counteract and overpower all darkness. He *is* the Light that redeemed us from the penalty of sin, restored us to the Father, and reconnected us to our destiny.

Chapter four presents our Heavenly Father's "last will and testament," detailing our spiritual inheritance through Jesus Christ. It presents an analysis of the destiny of believers as it relates to our position as *sons of God*. This chapter explains how God made us fit and acceptable, through the Blood of Jesus, to be His heirs and to receive our portion of the inheritance. We can rejoice, knowing that since we are His sons, everything He has belongs to us; for that is the way God planned it (Galatians 4:7b).

Beginning with chapter five, we delve deeper into the manifestations of God's glory. This chapter traces Jesus' steps from His sufferings at Calvary to the fullness and magnificence of His glory at His resurrection. By reliving the agony and victory of Jesus' last days, we gain strength, and are better prepared to travel the path to our destiny.

Chapter six examines how believers have authority, in the Name of Jesus Christ, to declare "His Glory" in every situation. This chapter shows how three Old Testament heroes—David, Daniel, and Nehemiah—operated in the power and authority of God's Word. There is an in-depth detailing of how we, too, can access God's power and have victory in every area of our lives.

Chapter seven explores how followers of Christ are destined to conform to His image (Romans 8:29). It identifies erroneous doctrines and teachings, which oftentimes are accepted as true. Acceptance of these doctrines and teachings impede the process of being transformed from "glory to glory." Many Christians are attempting to create "gray" areas and do not accept the reality of the consequences of sin. However, this chapter makes no mistake about it—right is still right and wrong is still wrong. We must be holy; for He is holy (1 Peter 1:16).

Chapter eight addresses how and why man was chosen—over all creation—to be crowned with God's glory and honor. It offers an analysis of the consequences of lucifer being ejected from Heaven, and his fierce opposition to mankind being the conduit of God's glory. This chapter also demonstrates how, when the adversary comes against us, he is repeating the same mistake he made with our Lord and Savior, Jesus Christ. When Jesus was crucified, His glory and honor did not diminish. They were magnified. Likewise, whatever the enemy means for bad, God will use it for our good; and His glory and honor will be magnified in our lives.

The Hebrew word *kavod,* often translated as "glory," might be more appropriately rendered "presence." Chapter nine discusses how in *His Presence,* believers are equipped, sustained, and blessed with everything needed to defeat the enemy and reach our divine destiny. It also explains how experiencing the *Shekinah* (manifested presence of God) leads us to our destination—the place where our lives glorify Him.

God is not only omnipresent, He is also omnipotent; and can manifest His power when, where, and however He chooses. In chapter ten, observed is the readily perceived, clearly visible, manifested power of God operating on behalf of His people. Chapter ten teaches how every principality, power, might, dominion, and name have been put under our Lord's feet, and under our feet (Psalm 8:6). This chapter demonstrates that when believers follow God's instructions, and strive to give Him the glory, nothing can prevent His purpose and plan from coming forth in our lives.

The final chapter emphasizes the need, and to some extent God's command, for believers to rest in Him. As we obey God's command to walk the path of destiny, He will give us His *shalom* (peace). In the abundance of His peace, nothing is missing or broken. Therefore, believers can live in expectation and not worry about our future. This chapter reminds us that the LORD will be with us always, and do whatever is needed for us to complete our journey.

The Word of God is the foundation for all my teachings; however, the Bible won't have much meaning if we don't relate it to our own lives. If you can personally apply the lessons in this book and see the outcomes, you shall partake of the glory that is coming to the Kingdom. Please understand this vital point: God's purpose and plan is not about us. It's all about His glory being revealed in the world. We are *destined for glory!*

ONE

DESTINY

Even every one that is called by my name:
for I have created him for my glory,
I have formed him; yea, I have made him.
(Isaiah 43:7)

O ur existence is not a coincidence, accident, or mistake. Every believer has a preordained purpose that is designed ultimately to bring forth God's will on the earth. *Destiny* is God's plan for our lives. When believers follow His plan, we can expect joy, success, and prosperity. Not following it can cause frustration, failure, and lack. Therefore, we must be determined, no matter what may come against us, to embrace *God's purpose and plan for our lives.*

As we pursue our destiny, it is important to understand that this journey is not about us. *It's all about God!* It's all about His purpose for mankind being fulfilled. He created us for His glory and as our destiny unfolds the magnificence, brilliance, and majesty of God shall be revealed through us.

To gain a deeper understanding of how the body of Christ is *Destined for Glory,* we need to start at the very beginning when God created man. God's eternal purpose is to be glorified and expressed through His Son, Jesus Christ, and through everyone who believes in Him. Because of sin, man was removed from his initial place in glory. However, the LORD has remained faithful to His plan for mankind and made a way for believers in Christ to fulfill our divine purpose. Let's go to Genesis, chapter 1, and begin our study on the destiny of the believer.

> *And God said, Let us make man in our*
> *image, after our likeness: and let them*
> *have dominion over the fish of the sea,*
> *and over the fowl of the air, and over the*
> *cattle, and over all the earth,*
> *and over every creeping thing*
> *that creepeth upon the earth.*
>
> *So God created man in his own image,*
> *in the image of God created he him;*
> *male and female created he them.*
> *(Genesis 1:26–27)*

First, it is important to note here that man initially was created *spiritually* in the image and likeness of God. Physical or "natural" man, whom God named Adam, did not come into existence until the second chapter of Genesis (verse 7). God formed a physical body or "earth suit" for man and breathed the breath of life into him. Then man became a living soul. Let's continue reading.

> *And the LORD God caused a deep sleep to*
> *fall upon Adam, and he slept:*
> *and he took one of his ribs, and*
> *closed up the flesh instead thereof;*
>
> *And the rib, which the LORD God*
> *had taken from man, made he a woman,*
> *and brought her unto the man.*
>
> *And Adam said, This is now bone*
> *of my bones, and flesh of my flesh:*
> *she shall be called Woman, because*
> *she was taken out of Man.*
>
> *Therefore shall a man leave his father*
> *and his mother, and shall cleave*
> *unto his wife: and they shall be one flesh.*
>
> *And they were both naked, the man and*
> *his wife, and were not ashamed.*
> *(Genesis 2:21–25)*

This passage describes how God provided Adam with a companion whom he called Woman. The man and his wife were completely naked, yet they were not ashamed because God's glory covered them. Adam and his wife were in total harmony with the LORD and all their needs are met. They were in position to fulfill their destiny. *Adam and his wife were firmly and perfectly connected to God, His purpose, and plan.*

17

The Enemy's Strategy

The adversary understands that as long as we stay connected to God and fulfill His purpose, God's glory *shall* be revealed. Therefore, satan's strategy, since the beginning when man was created, has been to separate us from our Creator *and* our destiny. The adversary knows that the more success he has in separating us from our destiny, the more God's glory will be diminished in our lives.

Sin separates mankind from the LORD. Satan is the originator of sin and introduced it to Adam and Eve in the Garden of Eden. In Genesis, chapter 3, we find the enemy setting up the woman to make a devastating mistake. Satan knew that if he could separate the wife from her husband, he had a good chance of separating them from God, and they would be in no position to give Him glory.

God did not give the man and woman many instructions with do's and don'ts. There was only one thing God told Adam not to do. In Genesis 2:16–17, God said:

*...Of every tree of the garden thou
mayest freely eat:*

*But of the tree of the knowledge
of good and evil, thou shalt not eat of it:
for in the day that thou eatest thereof
thou shalt surely die.*

The devil talked to the woman about what God said. Genesis 3:1–6 details the conversation between satan and Eve. It reads:

...And he said unto the woman,
Yea, hath God said, Ye shall not eat
of every tree of the garden?

And the woman said unto the serpent,
We may eat of the fruit
of the trees of the garden:

But of the fruit of the tree which is
in the midst of the garden, God hath said,
Ye shall not eat of it, neither
shall ye touch it, lest ye die.

And the serpent said unto the woman,
Ye shall not surely die:

For God doth know that in the day ye eat
thereof, then your eyes shall be opened,
and ye shall be as gods,
knowing good and evil.

And when the woman saw that the tree
was good for food, and that it was
pleasant to the eyes, and a tree
to be desired to make one wise,
she took of the fruit thereof,
and did eat, and gave also unto her
husband with her; and he did eat.

Satan said, in essence, "You can eat that forbidden fruit. The only reason God told you not to eat it is because He doesn't want you to be like Him." Believing satan's lie, the woman ate the fruit of the tree and persuaded her husband to eat also.

Deceived by satan, the woman desired to do the one thing God had forbidden. Genesis 2:17b says, "For in the day that thou eatest thereof thou shalt surely die." Adam and Eve sinned against God and immediately suffered the penalty.

Spiritual Disconnection

And the eyes of them both were opened,
and they knew that they were naked;
and they sewed fig leaves together,
and made themselves aprons.
(Genesis 3:7)

In Genesis 2:25, Adam and Eve were naked, but they were not ashamed; for they were connected to God, and His glory covered them in every way. However, after yielding to the temptation of satan, they saw their own nakedness and tried to cover themselves.

The serpent used a moment when Eve was alone to plant an idea in her mind that was against the purpose, plan, and will of God. When Eve ate the forbidden fruit, satan succeeded in temporarily separating her from Adam. As she offered the fruit for her husband to eat, I believe that Adam fully understood the consequences. However, as an act of commitment to remain with his bride, he also ate the forbidden fruit. Consequently, together, they were spiritually disconnected from God. Let's continue reading Genesis, chapter 3.

*And they heard the voice of the LORD God
walking in the garden in the cool of the
day: and Adam and his wife hid
themselves from the presence of the LORD
God amongst the trees of the garden.*

*And the LORD God called unto Adam,
and said unto him, Where art thou?*

*And he said, I heard thy voice in the
garden, and I was afraid, because
I was naked; and I hid myself.*

*And he said, Who told thee that thou
wast naked? Hast thou eaten of the tree,
whereof I commanded thee that
thou shouldest not eat?*
(Genesis 3:8–11)

Adam knew he had eaten what God forbade. As God began to question Adam, he said, in effect, "God this is not my fault! This woman you gave me brought me this stuff and I ate it!"

Satan's goal was accomplished when Adam ate from the tree of the knowledge of good and evil: man became separated from his destiny. Christians must realize that the plans God has for us are greater than anything we could ever imagine. Before contemplating doing anything contrary to God's Word and instructions, we should be aware of the loss and the cost.

Some carnal-minded Christians will do things that are not pleasing to the LORD and think little of it (Romans

8:6–8). These people do not understand that by engaging in activity contrary to God's Word, they have allowed the enemy to separate them from the promises of God. Our Heavenly Father has destined many wonderful things for us! He has ordered blessings that are ready to be released. Why would anyone allow himself or herself to be separated from what God preordained for their lives? *It is not worth it.*

Moses faced more temptations and adversities than most of us will ever see, but he realized nothing the enemy offered was worth missing out on his destiny. Hebrews 11:24–25 reads:

> *By faith Moses, when he was*
> *come to years, refused to be called*
> *the son of Pharaoh's daughter;*
>
> *Choosing rather to suffer affliction*
> *with the people of God, than to enjoy*
> *the pleasures of sin for a season;*

Moses said that he would rather suffer affliction with the people of God than enjoy the *pleasures of sin;* that is, doing wrong things that are against the Word of God. By faith, Moses embraced God's purpose and plan for his life.

How Are You Operating?

Christians have a choice: operate in the *light*, which is living according to the Word of God, or operate in darkness. We can choose to operate according to the mandate of the Kingdom of God or the mandate of the principalities of hell. There is no in-between.

There are people who claim to be part of the body of Christ but do not understand that every time they sin, they are disconnecting themselves from their God-given destiny. When they choose to steal, lie, or sow discord, they are saying, "I am willing to disconnect myself from what God had in mind for my life from the foundation of the world. I am willing to throw it all away for this pleasure."

Hold onto Destiny

None of us is exempt from the adversary's attacks. His strategy is to load us down with problems, situations, and trials so that we will let go of what God has declared. The adversary does not want us to reach our divine destination. But the Word of God lets us know we already have the victory, through our Lord and Savior Jesus Christ (1 Corinthians 15:57). We have overcome the enemy by the Blood of the Lamb, and by the word of our testimony (Revelation 12:11).

Our victory begins in the spirit realm. Even when everything seems to be going wrong, you must know that in the spirit, the battle is already won. Your destiny is not determined by your current circumstances. You might have money to pay your bills or you might not. You might have friends when you need them or you might not. Regardless of what is happening in the natural realm, *hold onto destiny!* God's purpose and plan for your life shall unfold and His glory will be revealed.

Love

Most people understand that *God is love* (1 John 4:8, 16). And he who abides in love, abides in God, and God in him. The problem is, we do not realize just how much He loves us. Our Father wants to show forth love to His children. He wants to embrace us daily and load us with the benefits of His will, purpose, and plan for our lives (Psalm 68:19).

Looking back at Genesis 3:8–9, we find God asking Adam, "Where art thou?" We know that God is omniscient and, therefore, knew exactly where Adam was located. The LORD called out to Adam because he was missing from the usual place where they fellowshipped and communed. Sin disrupted the intimate relationship Adam shared with the LORD. Adam no longer walked in his destiny and became separated from his Heavenly Father.

Many of us have testimonies of the trials, illnesses, and disappointments we have gone through. These testimonies prove that the enemy's plans to separate us from God's love failed. If satan had his way, none of us would live to see a new day. If we did not understand the spiritual reality of our destiny, the pressures of life would have us crying without a clue of what to do. But when we view our circumstances with spiritual eyes, we place them in the proper perspective and look forward to destiny.

It's all about God! He created us to give Himself glory. When we worship and praise God no matter what is happening in our lives, His manifested power will move mightily upon us. We have no fear because we know that God loves us and our destiny is in His hand.

The pleasures of sin for a season in no way compare to the destiny God has declared for our lives. We cannot allow anything to separate us from Him. The apostle Paul wrote:

> *For I am persuaded, that neither death,*
> *nor life, nor angels, nor principalities,*
> *nor powers, nor things present,*
> *nor things to come,*
>
> *Nor height, nor depth, nor any other*
> *creature, shall be able to separate us*
> *from the love of God, which is in*
> *Christ Jesus our Lord.*
> *(Romans 8:38–39)*

The enemy thought he had succeeded in separating mankind from our destiny, but as we will see in the upcoming chapters of this book, he was greatly mistaken. God provided the answer for every believer— His Name is Jesus. We are more than conquerors through Christ Jesus our Lord who loves us (v. 37).

In chapter two, we will delve more deeply while studying the destiny God declared for His people before the foundation of the world. Isaiah 55:11 says, "So shall my word be that goeth forth out of my mouth: it shall not return unto me void, but it shall accomplish that which I please, and it shall prosper in the thing where-to I sent it." This means that your destiny shall come to pass. Be determined to fulfill God's purpose and plan for your life. Nothing can stop us and no one can hold us back because we are *destined for glory!*

TWO

BEFORE THE FOUNDATION OF THE WORLD

Blessed be the God and Father of our Lord
*Jesus Christ, **who hath blessed us***
with all spiritual blessings
in heavenly places in Christ:

According as he hath chosen us in him
before the foundation of the world,
that we should be holy and
without blame before him in love:
(Ephesians 1:3–4)

P eople of destiny are *blessed,* that is, empowered to prosper, equipped to succeed, and positioned to live in abundance. Verse 3 of the above Scripture passage states that we are blessed with *all* spiritual blessings. The apostle Paul further explains that God *hath blessed* us. "Hath blessed" is past tense, so what Paul is really saying is that we are already blessed. It is a spiritual fact—finished and accomplished. Some of our blessings have manifested, but many of them are waiting for us in the spirit realm. Be encouraged, because there is an appointed time for a release from the spirit to the natural. These spiritual blessings are part of God's purpose and plan for our lives and we are destined to receive them.

Chosen

In this chapter, we will study how God established our election and destiny in Christ *before the foundation of the world* (Ephesians 1:4). We will discuss how our destiny has been declared before the world began. Our end was set before creation. We were selected to be a consistent presentation of God and His love upon the earth. He knows us by name (Exodus 33:17) and has ordered every step we shall take to give Him glory and honor.

Ephesians 1:5–6 says:

> *Having predestinated us unto the adoption*
> *of children by Jesus Christ to himself,*
> *according to the good pleasure of his will,*
>
> *To the praise of the glory of his grace,*
> *wherein he hath made us*
> *accepted in the beloved.*

The *Amplified Bible* reads:

> *For He foreordained us (destined us,*
> *planned in love for us) to be adopted*

*(revealed) as His own children through
Jesus Christ, in accordance with the
purpose of His will [because it pleased Him
and was His kind intent]—*

*[So that we might be] to the praise and the
commendation of His glorious grace (favor
and mercy), which He so freely bestowed
on us in the Beloved.*

Predestinated tells of a future outcome that was pre-determined. Our future was *foreordained* (chosen and appointed beforehand) by God in heavenly places before we were conceived in our mother's womb (Jeremiah 1:5). The LORD knows each of us personally and has selected us for Himself. We were destined to belong to the Father through Jesus Christ.

Before the beginning began, God structured the world so that His children would be able to carry out His will in earth, as it is in Heaven. God is the great architect and planner of the universe and designer of its destiny. He is also the constructor and builder of our lives. He *destined us for glory.* It pleases the LORD to provide freely everything we need to accomplish His purpose and plan.

Show Forth His Praise

*This people have I formed for myself;
they shall show forth my praise.
(Isaiah 43:21)*

There is a big difference between people who understand that their lives are destined to give God praise (glory) and those who don't. Let me give you an example. My church, *Word of Deliverance Ministries for the World, Inc.* in Forest Park, Ohio was in special prayer for a young lady in our congregation who was diagnosed with a brain tumor. She was scheduled for surgery and asked for our prayers. Surgical procedures are always a serious matter, but when the brain is involved, the situation becomes even more critical.

This was not the time to collapse because of the surgeon's report. When someone is facing a "test" of this magnitude, those interceding on the person's behalf must have strong confidence and faith in God and His Word. We stood knowing that Jesus was wounded for our transgressions and bruised for our iniquities…and by His stripes we are healed (Isaiah 53:5). We believed that this young lady was destined to be healed. We prayed that the LORD would be with her, keep her, and bring her out! We continued praising God and trusted that He was going to give this young lady the victory.

I had planned to stop by the hospital the day of her surgery to offer my support to the family. They had informed me that the operation would take several hours, so I really was not expecting to visit or see her that day. Upon arriving at the hospital, her family told me she was out of surgery and in recovery. When the surgeons opened the area where the tumor was, it just "plopped out" and they closed her back up.

This young lady was out of the hospital in record time. Shortly after, when she returned to church, her appearance was so bright and healthy that no one would have known she had just undergone brain surgery. She hadn't lost any weight, had full use of her limbs, and had no speech deficits. God had predetermined her miraculous outcome for His glory.

This lady understood her destiny. She illustrates the fact that when *people of destiny* face these types of crisis, we can expect a miracle and God will get glory before the eyes of everyone! We were created to *show forth His praise!*

Press toward the Mark

The LORD wants His people to be victorious because this gives Him glory. He wants to show us new and greater things and take us to new and greater places. Unfortunately, some people whom the world characterizes as successful believe they have "arrived." They have become content with their professional status and think that since their life is so wonderful, there could not possibly be more in store for them.

However, others like myself know that this is not a season to be complacent, but rather a time to move forward in the high calling of God. Paul provides a good example of the attitude Christians should have. He tells the Philippians:

*Brethren, I count not myself to have
apprehended: but this one thing I do,
forgetting those things which are behind,
and reaching forth unto
those things which are before,*

*I press toward the mark for the prize of
the high calling of God in Christ Jesus.
(Philippians 3:13–14)*

As great as Paul was in establishing churches and promoting the Kingdom of God, the apostle knew he had not "arrived." Paul said, "I count not myself to have apprehended." Paul understood that he had not yet become or done everything God destined for him. He also recognized the importance of forgetting those things which are behind, because dwelling on past experiences and memories can be a distraction. The apostle focused on reaching forth unto his destiny and encouraged the church at Philippi to "be thus minded,"—pressing toward the mark for the prize of the high calling of God in Christ Jesus.

Under Construction

Sometimes as we press toward the mark, our lives can seem cluttered and messy—like the early phase of a construction site. Debris is scattered everywhere and nothing looks in place. In this stage of the construction project, it is often difficult to visualize how the final structure will look.

To provide a clearer picture of what is going on and what will be in the future, contractors will sometimes place big pictorial signs with an artist's rendering of the building at the edge of the property. These signs are designed to offer reassurance that the dust, disorder, dirt, and detours are only temporary because in a short time this ugly, messy construction site is going to be a beautiful structure for all to behold!

Even when your life seems to be in the early stages of construction and messy, you are still *destined for glory.* Be confident—God builds and develops us as we pursue His purpose and plan for our lives. Paul writes in Philippians 1:6

> *Being confident of this very thing, that he which hath begun a good work in you will perform it until the day of Jesus Christ:*

Never allow the enemy to intimidate or discourage you about negative situations. Your future was foreordained *before the foundation of the world,* so keep on pressing because the LORD is still working on you!

A Holy Calling

2 Timothy 1:9 says:

> *Who hath saved us, and called us with an holy calling, not according to our works, but according to his own purpose and grace, which was given us in Christ Jesus before the world began...*

33

The *Living Bible* says it this way:

> *It is he who saved us and chose us for his*
> *holy work, not because we deserved it but*
> *because that was his plan long before*
> *the world began—to show his love and*
> *kindness to us through Christ.*

Every believer should understand and accept the call God placed on our lives before the world began. He chose and consecrated us for His purpose, not because of our talents, our gifts, not even our works. The LORD called us to show forth His love and kindness. We were given a *holy calling* through Christ Jesus. So it really doesn't matter how low you are, because His grace is sufficient (2 Corinthians 12:9). God will raise you and keep you on the path to your destiny!

Declaring the End from the Beginning

> *Remember the former things of old:*
> *for I am God, and there is none else;*
> *I am God, and there is none like me,*
>
> *Declaring the end from the beginning,*
> *and from ancient times the things*
> *that are not yet done,*
> *saying, My counsel shall stand, and*
> *I will do all my pleasure:*
> *(Isaiah 46:9–10)*

In this passage of Scripture, the prophet Isaiah is talking about *destiny*. As we meditate on our destiny we must remember and fully recognize who God is, not who we are. He is sovereign and there is no one like Him!

The Almighty conveyed through the prophet that our end has been declared from the beginning and His plan for our lives shall stand. As the Creator, He does whatever He pleases and purposes in His mind. God's Word over our lives cannot be blotted out or erased. He declared our spiritual blessings before the foundation of the world and they shall come to pass.

Don't Worry About Anything

It takes a mature relationship with the LORD to say, "I am not worried," while our physical senses tell us otherwise. When we truly trust God, we will experience a peaceful rest in Him that will not allow us to worry about anything.

Believers find it easier to enter into God's rest when we know that we are living according to His Word and instructions. Christians are called with a *holy* calling; therefore we must be holy. Committing to a lifestyle that glorifies and pleases God must be at the core of every Christian's heart. Our Heavenly Father wants His children to walk in obedience to Him living devoted and consecrated lives based on His *written* Word—The Bible. We must be holy in our homes, at our jobs, in our cars, and on our telephones. No matter how insignificant the situations or circumstances might seem, we must always conduct ourselves in a manner that gives God glory (1 Corinthians 10:31).

Mature Christians learn to avoid things that are unholy because we understand the importance of having an intimate relationship with a holy God. The blessings of God are manifested as we live according to His Word in the beauty of holiness, and stay connected to the plan of God for our lives.

Stay on Course

Most of us remember when we were small children how our parents would hold our hands while crossing the street or shopping at the store. They would reach down and hold our small hand in theirs so that we would not get lost or stray too far from them. If we started pulling and trying to go in the wrong direction, our father or mother would tug on our hand and lead us in the right direction.

Our Heavenly Father guides His children similarly. When we attempt to stray, He tugs at us to get our attention and guides us in the right direction. We do not want to tempt God by trying to pull in a different direction, one contrary to His plan.

As we intensify our submission to God, His favor and benefits will be loaded upon us daily (Psalm 68:19). We must say in our hearts, *"I want to please God in every-thing I do; I am walking with Him, and I must stay on the course He planned for me."*

The destiny God has planned for us is glorious and grand! Any obstacle we might face is just another opportunity for a testimony of how we made it through. The LORD is manufacturing so many blessings in our lives and He's doing it in such a great way that it is going to capture the world's attention.

God's people are called to make a difference in our communities, cities, nation, and in the world. God is going to receive great and marvelous glory from our lives. Keep your head up and hands lifted because you are on your way. Remember that your destiny was spoken before the foundation of the world. The Psalmist writes:

> *For ever, O LORD, thy word*
> *is settled in heaven.*
> *(Psalm 119:89)*

The LORD'S Word is forever settled in Heaven and His counsel cannot be moved, changed, or rearranged. God said it, and it is so! Are you excited about your future? Are you ready to fulfill God's plan for your life? Let's continue on this journey of understanding our destiny.

THREE

LET THERE BE LIGHT

But God hath revealed them unto us by his
Spirit: for the Spirit searcheth all things,
yea, the deep things of God.
(1 Corinthians 2:10)

Pursuing *destiny* takes us into the deep things of God. The message in this book is not for people who are insincere and nonchalant about the things God has prepared for us. People with this mindset might not be able to receive this word. This message is for true believers of the Lord Jesus Christ who are earnestly searching and seeking to fulfill God's call on their lives.

Today's generation is living in a time when events such as the Attack on America on September 11, 2001, turmoil in the Middle East, terrorism, wars, and rumors of wars have put fear and uncertainty into the hearts of many people. This is not the time for believers to have any doubt about their destiny. The body of Christ must understand that even when there is perplexity on every side, God's purpose and plan for our lives remains set. Remember the Psalmist's words in the previous chapter where he encourages us that God's Word is forever settled in Heaven (Psalm 119:89).

It is impossible to comprehend the depths of our divine destiny without taking a further look at the fall of man from his spiritual position in God. Adam's sin presented a serious dilemma. As we saw earlier, his disobedience separated mankind not only from God, but also from our destiny. Yet, the Bible clearly states that we were created for God's glory and that His people shall show forth His praise (Isaiah 43:7, 21).

Adam's decision to disobey certainly did not catch Almighty God by surprise. Remember our Creator is omniscient and knew Adam would sin before it ever happened. Since God declared the end from the beginning, He foreknew the obstacles we would face. *Jehovah-jireh*, our provider, has already made a way of escape from every obstacle that would stop us from obtaining our destiny. The LORD will not leave us nor forsake us.

The Gap Theory

To understand God's answer for man's dilemma, we must return to the first book in the Bible. Let's read Genesis 1:1–2:

40

*In the beginning God created
the heaven and the earth.*

*And the earth was without form, and void;
and darkness was upon the face of the
deep. And the Spirit of God moved upon
the face of the waters.*

God is perfect and does everything in excellence. When heaven and earth were created in Genesis 1:1, they were in a state of perfection. Yet, when we get to Genesis 1:2, the earth is in a chaotic state.

Many theologians believe that lucifer and a third part of the angels (Revelation 12:4, 9) were expelled from Heaven in the period between Genesis 1:1 and Genesis 1:2. This interpretation is often referred to as the *gap theory.* Lucifer and the other fallen angels' descent from Heaven created a dark empty and chaotic condition. Genesis 1:2 tells us, "The earth was without form and void." The earth was in a state of confusion and covered with darkness.

The Book of Isaiah may provide some insight into the events which could have occurred between Genesis 1:1 and Genesis 1:2. Isaiah 14:12–14 says:

*How art thou fallen from heaven,
O Lucifer, son of the morning!
How art thou cut down to the ground,
which didst weaken the nations!*

41

*For thou hast said in thine heart, I will
ascend into heaven, I will exalt my throne
above the stars of God: I will sit also
upon the mount of the congregation,
in the sides of the north:*

*I will ascend above the heights of the
clouds; I will be like the most High.*

Apparently lucifer said in his heart, *I am going to exalt
myself in Heaven and be just as great as God.* Can you
imagine lucifer holding a board meeting with several
fellow angels who agreed with him and said, "Yes,
lucifer, you can do that." Soon after, lucifer and his
cohorts were thrown out of Heaven with such force the
scene looked like lightning bolts (Luke 10:18). God
probably said something like, "You and your buddies,
get out! Hit the road, Jack!"

Let's look again at Genesis 1:2. It says that the earth was
without form and void. This might be better understood by saying the earth became a place of confusion
and emptiness. This verse goes on to say that there
was darkness upon the *face of the deep* and the Spirit
of God moved upon the *face of the waters.*

At first glance, one could assume that the darkness
upon the *face of the deep* was covering the face of the
waters, upon which the spirit of God was moving.
Darkness in this passage of Scripture refers to destruction, death, ignorance, misery, sorrow, and wickedness. I believe this darkness upon the face of the deep
was brought about by lucifer in an attempt to cover

the plan of God or what is referred to in 1 Corinthians 2:10 as the deep things of God.

The devil brings darkness to everything he touches. At one time this fallen cherub (Ezekiel 28:13–19) had the privilege to observe the workings of the LORD at the highest levels. Lucifer understood that the divine purpose for all creation was to glorify God. When lucifer landed in the earthly realm, obstructing the glory of God became his number one goal.

Let me reiterate this point: when the Bible speaks of darkness being upon the *face of the deep,* I believe it is referring to the glory and plan of God being obscured. Lucifer's darkness attempted to cover the divine purpose and will of God in the earth. However, the Spirit of God was yet moving upon the face of the waters.

God's Answer

> And God said, **Let there be light:**
> and there was light.
> (Genesis 1:3)

Before the foundation of the world, God had provided the answer to the spiritual darkness that covered the earth. The LORD knew iniquity would be found in lucifer before it entered his imagination. When God said, "Let there be light," every evil deed the devil ever planned had a divine answer to counteract it. Hallelujah! There is deliverance in that light and we thank God for it.

This may seem like a simple statement, but a deeper study and revelation of what happened when God spoke these words which brought forth light confirms that it is one of the most profound and powerful declarations in the Bible.

> *And God saw the light, that it was good:*
> *and God divided the light*
> *from the darkness.*
> *(Genesis 1:4)*

Reading further in Genesis 1:4 we see where God said to Himself, "This is good." This light was more than just a flash or temporary break from the darkness. The light of Genesis 1:3 counteracted every devastation of Genesis 1:2. When God said, "Let there be light" divine order was restored; the devil was defeated, and we were blessed with all spiritual blessings in heavenly places (Ephesians 1:3). That light brought salvation to mankind. That light established our destiny in the spirit, which manifests now and forever.

Many people have read Genesis 1:3 numerous times and assumed it is describing the creation of the sun and moon. But if you carefully read Genesis 1:16-19 you will read that God did not create the sun and the moon until the fourth day. Therefore, light in passages Genesis 1:3–4 is not referring to the sun or moon. I propose to you that this light is the Son who the prophet Isaiah said would be called Wonderful, Counsellor, The Mighty God, The Everlasting Father, The Prince of Peace (Isaiah 9:6): Jesus Christ, our Lord and Savior.

Jesus Is the Light

In the beginning was the Word,
and the Word was with God,
and the Word was God.

The same was in the beginning with God.

All things were made by him;
and without him was not
any thing made that was made.

In him was life; and the life
was the light of men.

And the light shineth in darkness;
and the darkness comprehended it not.
(John 1:1–5)

Let me show you a brief but closer comparative analysis, which demonstrates that the light referred to in Genesis 1, is the same light, Jesus Christ, in John 1. In Genesis, chapter 1, we read about the creation of Heaven and earth while in John 1 we learn about the pre-existence of Christ who was in the beginning with God. The Book of Genesis records the realm of creation beginning with day one, when light was created; day two, the firmament; day three, land and seas; day four, the sun and moon; day five, the birds and fish; and day six, animals and man. In the Book of John, we find that Jesus was not only in the beginning, but verse 3 tells us He made all things. As previously stated, Genesis 1:2 talks about darkness, which covered the face of the deep. In verse three we read that God dispelled darkness by speaking the word let there be light and there was light.

The Book of John emphasizes the deity of Jesus and His oneness with God. According to John 1:1, the Word was in the beginning with God and was God. John 1:14 says:

And the Word was made flesh, and dwelt among us, (and we beheld his glory, the glory as of the only begotten of the Father,) full of grace and truth.

Jesus is the ultimate expression of God's Word. So back in Genesis 1:3 when God said, "Let there be light," this light dispelled and cancelled out everything birthed by darkness such as destruction, death, ignorance, sorrow, misery, and wickedness. John 1:5 declares the light shines in, and supersedes the darkness. This is the same light spoken of in Genesis 1:3. Jesus is God's Word made flesh (John 1:14). He brings forth light that shines in darkness. *Jesus is the light.* Our Lord and Savior, Jesus Christ is the light of the world whom all believers must embrace to counteract and overpower all darkness.

John bare witness of him, and cried, saying, This was he of whom I spake, He that cometh after me is preferred before me: for he was before me.
(John 1:15, The Living Bible)

It is important for us to have this Word in our spirits. We must be confident of the truth that Jesus Christ is the ultimate expression of God's spoken Word. Because of Jesus Christ's blood, our sins are forgiven and we are restored into fellowship with Father God. He fulfilled His divine purpose as Savior of the world when He destroyed the works of satan (Matthew 1:21, John 4:42, 1 John 3:8). We must also realize that through Jesus Christ we have been called out of darkness into His marvelous light. 1 Peter 2:9 says:

> *But ye are a chosen generation,*
> *a royal priesthood, an holy nation,*
> *a peculiar people;*
> *that ye should shew forth*
> *the praise, of him who*
> *hath called you out of darkness*
> *into his marvellous light.*

Follow the Light

> *Then spake Jesus again unto them, saying,*
> *I am the light of the world: he that*
> *followeth me shall not walk in darkness,*
> *but shall have the light of life.*
> *(John 8:12)*

You can choose to either walk in the light or in darkness. It does not matter if someone has a license to preach, teach and carries a leather briefcase or big family Bible; to fulfill your destiny you must follow the Light of the world. The Word of God must control, lead, and guide your steps. As you walk in the Light, God's purpose and plan for your life will unfold.

Jesus is the Light and the Word and He dwells in us (John 1:1–15). The Psalmist states that thy word *is* a lamp unto my feet, and a light unto my path (Psalm 119:105). His Light empowers and guides us along our path of destiny. Before the beginning began, God provided the answer to keep us on course...*Follow the Light, Follow Jesus!*

In the next chapter, we will examine what it means to be sons, and therefore heirs, through Jesus Christ, to the Kingdom of God. We will see how our Heavenly Father wants us to fulfill our destiny and enjoy the full benefits of being part of His royal family. Nothing can compare to the inheritance God has established for His children. Come join me for this reading of our Lord's last will and Testament.

FOUR

HEIRS

*...And since we are his sons
everything he has belongs to us,
for that is the way God planned.
(Galatians 4:7b, The Living Bible)*

In the above Scripture passage, we have a verse from Paul. Here, the apostle is teaching on spiritual inheritance to the believers in Galatia. In this letter, the apostle focuses particularly on three main themes in this letter to the Galatians: liberty from the law through Jesus Christ; redemption from the penalty of sin and death through the Blood of Jesus Christ; and reassurance of the eternal heirship to the Kingdom of God, also through Christ Jesus.

Chapter 4 of Galatians is very encouraging to the body of Christ. Its message is clear: God sent His only begotten Son, Jesus Christ, to redeem us from the bondage of sin. It is because of the "finished work" at Calvary that we have been adopted into the family of

God. This adoption made us joint-heirs with Jesus Christ and heirs of God; so everything He has belongs to us. John 1:11–12 supports this spiritual fact that Jesus Christ was not accepted by His own (Jews); but all who received Him and believed on His Name were given the right to become sons of God.

Sonship

For as many as are led by the Spirit of
God, they are the sons of God.
(Romans 8:14)

What an honor and privilege it is to be called the sons of God. Our Heavenly Father does not want us ignorant of what the future holds. He desires us, His children, to fully understand our destiny as well as our sonship. As I stated in another book God honored me to author, *The Blessing of Commitment: Releasing Wealth and Riches into Your Life*, sonship in Scripture does not denote one's gender. Galatians 3:28 declares that there is neither male nor female in Christ Jesus—we are one in Him. Sonship denotes our position as His children and our posture as being humbly submitted to His rule, power, and authority.

The Inheritance of the Saints

For this cause we also, since the day we
heard it, do not cease to pray for you,
and to desire that ye might be filled

> *with the knowledge of his will*
> *in all wisdom and spiritual understanding;*
>
> *That ye might walk worthy of the Lord*
> *unto all pleasing, being fruitful*
> *in every good work, and increasing*
> *in the knowledge of God;*
>
> *Strengthened with all might, according*
> *to his glorious power, unto all patience*
> *and longsuffering with joyfulness;*
>
> *Giving thanks unto the Father,*
> *which hath made us meet to be partakers*
> *of the inheritance of the saints in light:*
> *(Colossians 1:9–12)*

In this Scripture passage, the apostle Paul prays for the believers to be completely endowed with the knowledge of God's will. As we grow more cognizant of His plan and His purpose for our lives, the end result should be pleasing to Him. Our walk or day-to-day conduct and behavior must be one that exemplifies our relationship with God. Just as Jesus' desire was to do the will of His Father, so must ours be. As sons of the true and living God and heirs to His Kingdom, we must be the apple of His eye and please Him in everything we do.

Colossians 1:12 is an exhortation to continuously give thanks to Father God, who has made us fit and acceptable, through the Blood of Jesus Christ to receive our portion of the inheritance. We must be absolutely clear in our heart that our Heavenly Father planned for us to be His heirs from the foundation of the world. We could never thank God enough for this gracious gift. I think of this honor to be heirs as a "grace gift" because we could never earn 'rights' to the Kingdom of God. We did nothing to deserve it but because of God's love, kindness, and favor, we are part of the royal family and, therefore, heirs to our Heavenly Father's Kingdom.

When individuals receive an inheritance, generally it is because someone has died and left it to them. According to Webster's Dictionary, to *inherit* means to receive by legal succession or will; or to come into possession. Because of the death of Jesus Christ, we received full spiritual and legal possession to the Kingdom of God. We are beneficiaries to all spiritual blessings in heavenly places in Christ Jesus (Ephesians 1:3).

God's Kingdom consists of an abundance of "good things." The prophet Daniel said, "And the time came that the saints possessed the kingdom" (Daniel 7:22). Paul, the apostle, told the church at Rome that the Kingdom of God was not meat and drink but righteousness, peace, and joy in the Holy Ghost (Romans 14:17). Then in the Book of Revelation, the apostle John describes its holiness, physical beauty, and wealth—full of gold, pearls and other precious stones (Revelation 21).

King Solomon has blessed us with much wisdom in the Book of Proverbs. However, let me draw your attention to a profound Scripture found in the Songs of Solomon. Chapter 8, verse 6 reads, "...Love is as strong as death." The Gospel of John says, "God so loved the world, that he gave his only begotten Son" (John 3:16). Later in the same book, Jesus said, "Greater love hath no man than this, that a man lay down his life for his friends" (John 15:13). Both of these Scriptures describe the agape love shown us from our Heavenly Father and His Son. Because of this unconditional love, we are joint-heirs with Christ, heirs of God, and therefore connected to our destiny.

In chapter three of this book, we looked closely at Genesis 1:2–3. Verse 2 speaks of darkness covering the face of the deep (remember that darkness here refers to death, destruction, misery, ignorance and sorrow), but thank God for speaking the words in verse 3. He said, "Let there be light!" Darkness no longer had dominion in the earth. The light spoken into existence counteracted every spirit associated with that darkness. We, as believers, have been delivered from the power of darkness and transferred into the Kingdom of His Son.

If you want peace in knowing your inheritance, you must receive your deliverance from sin through the Blood of Jesus Christ and become grounded and settled in the hope of the gospel (good news of our Lord and Savior Jesus Christ) (Colossians 1:23). Too many people come to church week after week and never gain a deeper understanding of God's purpose and plan for their lives. If individuals are not aware of their connection to the Kingdom, they can easily fall away.

If you do not understand your destiny, the moment the devil says, "You aren't going to be healed" or "You'll never have peace," you will be tempted to say, "He's right." Be careful not to accept what the enemy says. When you understand your destiny, you realize that you are connected to God's divine purpose and plan. This is the point at which you put yourself in agreement with the Word of God, and receive your inheritance.

Destiny Prevails Over Affliction

But the more they afflicted them,
the more they multiplied and grew.
And they were grieved
because of the children of Israel.
(Exodus 1:12)

If someone is going to let go, sit down, and give up before obtaining what God has declared for his or her life, it is generally during times of affliction. When life presents pain, sorrow, hardship and heartaches, one could easily say, "I quit". Yet historically, as we see in Exodus 1:12, the more God's people were afflicted, the more they increased and expanded. They did not give up, cave in, or quit during these times of affliction.

Think about that for a moment. The children of Israel were people of destiny. Their end was predetermined. God established a set purpose in them before the foundation of the world.

Going back to Genesis 15:13, God told Abram that his seed would be afflicted as slaves in a strange land for 400 years. He also foretold His judgment on the Egyptians and of the great wealth with which the children of Israel would obtain. God had a set time for His children to be delivered (Exodus 12:40–42, 51). No one could cut them off from the promises of God. The enemy has no weapon in his arsenal that is capable of stopping God's children from reaching their ordained destination.

Bigger and Bigger

Our own doubts and fears can cause us to live defeated lives. This is why Christians must be grounded and settled in the faith. Doubts and fears are erased when we know God's Word and stand on what He has declared.

The enemy afflicts us with issues designed to discourage us and make us want to quit trusting God. But when we have the Word inside of us, the adversary is in for quite a surprise. The devil thought he had us "down for the count," but the next time he takes a look he'll see that we've gotten bigger and bigger!

Our afflictions can actually cause us to spiritually increase and expand. The thought of this should bless you. Instead of being destroyed, you have grown. You've grown bigger, wiser, and more intelligent in spiritual things. You now have more knowledge about the faithfulness of God as a deliverer, and a personal testimony that He will keep your mind in perfect peace.

The enemy wants to wear us down, and when individuals do not understand their destiny, he will be successful in doing it. When the devil turns up the heat, many will attempt to return to the familiar and predictable ways of the world. It's not that these individuals do not realize that the world they left behind was a terrible place. The problem is, they do not understand their destiny. But the man who knows he is *destined for glory* will say, "This situation is just helping me to grow. I'm getting bigger and bigger."

The devil's tactics are proof that he really does not understand the Word of God. The enemy may know the Word, but he doesn't understand it. He can't understand truth, because lies and deception dominate his nature. When spiritual truth is known with understanding, it penetrates our very soul. 1 Corinthians 2:8 tells us, *"Which none of the princes of this world knew: for had they known it, they would not have crucified the Lord of glory."* If Jesus' opponents had known the truth of His identity, they would have left Him alone. Had the enemy known that Jesus' Calvary experience would bring salvation to mankind and multiply and grow the Kingdom of God, he truly would have left Christ alone!

The Believers' Heritage

Abounding and increasing during times of adversity is the heritage of all believers. Instead of weakening us, afflictions make us stronger. A very old, yet true song believers sang years ago entitled *Through It All,* has relevance for us today.

THROUGH IT ALL
(André Crouch)

I've had many tears and sorrow,
I've had questions for tomorrow,
there've been times I didn't know
right from wrong,
but in every situation
God gave blessed consolation,
that my trials come
*to only make me **strong.***

So I thank God for the mountains,
and I thank Him for the valleys,
and I thank Him for the storms
He's brought me through,
for if I've never had a problem,
I'd never know that God
could solve them,
I'd never know what faith
in His Word could do.

Through it all, Through it all,
I've learned to trust in Jesus,
I've learned to trust in God.
Through it all, through it all
I've learned to depend upon His Word.

This song reminds us that anytime the enemy tries to press us down, continue to trust in God's Word. Adversities make us better. Unfortunately, when some people go through storms, they start "tripping." They get nervous and start panicking. However, those who understand their connection to destiny realize the enemy is just being used to give us a new testimony. Glory to God Almighty!

When I was afflicted with sickness and the doctors didn't know what to do, God healed me. Now I can testify that God is a healer. When people make it through an experience where they had no idea how things would turn out, they come forth with a testimony that God made a way. Yes, as heirs to the Kingdom of God, healing and provision are part of our inheritance as believers.

The Fellowship of the Believers

One of the great things about fellowshipping with believers is that we get to see one another grow. Some of us were in pitiful situations with one trouble after another. While you were overcoming that situation and got the victory, others saw you getting stronger and better. Your blessings multiplied; your faith increased, and your trust in God grew deeper. What the devil meant for your destruction, God used for your construction. *The devil should have left you alone!"*

Exodus 1:12b reads:

> *...and they were grieved
> because of the children of Israel.*

They, in the above Scripture refers to the Egyptians, the hard task masters. The fact that the children of Israel increased and expanded caused the Egyptians to become vexed and alarmed. The Egyptians were disgusted!

Many of us are grieving the enemy. He gets frustrated when, after all we have been through, we still have joy! We have caused the enemy to be confused and upset. He meant for us to be grieved, but he's the one grieving because we still have our praise! We can still lift our hands and say, "Thank you Jesus!"

It's Yours

We should give our Lord and Savior glory in everything we do because with Him all things are possible (Mark 9:23). Without Him we can do nothing (John 15:5). That is why there is no need to get upset when people tell you, "Oh, you can't do that." If God destined you to do it, you will. If God said you would have it, you will. If God planned something for your life, it shall come to pass. Regardless of how the situation looks, it's yours!

The LORD did not need a board meeting with a majority vote to declare your inheritance. No one else's opinion or permission was required. God all by Himself made the decision to bless you and make you an heir through Jesus Christ. We do not have to worry about being in the most popular club, crowd, or clique because whatever God decided, shall be done. When God said, "I am going to bless you," it was done—*you were blessed!*

Destiny's Child

God has certain expectations of the life of destiny's child. One of the requirements is living a life that glorifies Him. You must guard your ears, eyes, and sanctify your tongue, always blessing the LORD. The blessings of God for you are too great to risk losing them. Value what God has declared for your life. None of the tricks of the enemy are new. He is still using the same old dumb junk he used over 2000 years ago. The devil targets people who are weak in their knowledge, understanding, and application of the Scriptures. He preys on those weak in their spirit. This is why we must allow the Word of God to mature us so that we won't fall for the enemy's tactics. As children of destiny, we must stay in position, to fulfill God's plan for our life.

A person does not have to be a theologian to know that this is the hour and day of the Church. The glory of God is being manifested in the body of Christ in such an awesome way that His glory will flow through everyone who is connected. God is able to do exceeding abundantly above all that we could ask or think, according to the power that is working in us (Ephesians 3:20).

The LORD operates in times and seasons. We are on the path—toward the fullness of what He declared for our lives from the foundation of the world. This is the day spoken of by the prophet Joel (Joel 2:28, Acts 2:17). The glory of God is being revealed in a new and magnificent way. Clothe yourself with the Word of God; pursue His destiny, and partake of the inheritance.

In chapter five, we will explore the glory of God more deeply. Who better to show us His glory than God the Son, Jesus Christ, the Lord of Glory (1 Corinthians 2:8)?

FIVE

SEVEN DAYS TO GLORY

*Was it not necessary and essentially fitting
that the Christ (the Messiah) should suffer
all these things before entering into His
glory (His majesty and splendor)?
(Luke 24:26, The Amplified Bible)*

My God-given assignment in this book is to encourage and place a *word* in your spirit that keeps you excited and focused on His glory being revealed in your life. As this word becomes firmly rooted in your heart, it will grow within you a hope that strengthens your faith in the Word of God.

Please remember that fulfilling God's purpose for your life requires a level of confidence at which you know beyond all doubt that everything God has declared shall come to pass. Even when your natural senses (touch, sight, hearing, smell, and taste) indicate it's impossible and the situation appears hopeless, stand

63

strong because you are going to make it. Your destiny does not have to make *sense* for God to make it *real* in your life! In this chapter, we will meditate on the last seven days of Jesus Christ's life on earth. We will discuss how it was necessary and acceptable in the sight of God for Jesus, His only begotten Son, to suffer before coming into His majesty.

Jesus Is Our Example

The Bible can be viewed as a roadmap for Christians to follow as they travel their path to destiny. It provides lessons illustrating everything necessary to accomplish God's will. There is no better example in Scripture of someone fulfilling God's purpose and plan than Jesus Christ. Our Lord and Savior experienced many storms, heartaches, and pain; however, He was always *destined for glory.* Jesus' destiny did not begin with His birth in Bethlehem; it began from the foundation of the world. Christ's destiny as well as ours was spoken before Heaven and earth were created.

Many people believe that their intelligence, luck, or genes determine their destiny. But Jeremiah 1:5 says, *"Before I formed thee in the belly I knew thee; and before thou camest forth out of the womb I sanctified thee, and I ordained thee a prophet unto the nations."* Jeremiah's destiny was "fixed" before he was conceived—not by man's hand, but by God Almighty. When people fully understand that God's purpose and plan for their lives is predetermined, they will not be discouraged because of situations such as an unacceptable socioeconomic status. Remember, when God established your destiny, there were no earthly limitations restricting Him.

I am not denying the difficulty believers have trying to stay encouraged. We are *spirits*, who possess *souls*, which are wrapped up in *flesh* (our bodies/our "earth-suits"). And, every now and then, our flesh will cause us to feel depressed over the issues of life. However, feeling down should last only for a moment, because the Word of God is *spirit* and therefore powerful enough to lift and remind us that our destiny is in place.

Christ's Destiny

In the first chapter of Matthew, we find the angel Gabriel, God's messenger, saying to Mary that she would bring forth a Son who shall be called Jesus, for He shall save His people from their sins. In Hebrews 9:12, we find that the blood of Jesus was necessary to redeem us from sin. In 1 John 3:8, we see that the Son of God, Jesus Christ, was manifested that He might *destroy* (make inoperable and ineffective) the works of the devil.

Genesis 3:15 describes the first Messianic Promise: the conflict between the serpent and the Seed of the woman. This promise assures us that her Seed would bruise the head of the serpent. Therefore, her Seed would have power, dominion, and authority over any adverse action presented by the serpent.

65

Jesus was destined to fulfill every Word spoken concerning the coming Messiah. Yet, when we look at the last week of His life, Jesus' destiny appears to grow darker and more distant. There are many lessons to be learned by studying what Jesus endured before entering into His glory. Let's go to the Book of Luke and examine the final days of Jesus' life on earth.

Day One

> *And he went into the temple, and began*
> *to cast out them that sold therein,*
> *and them that bought;*
>
> *Saying unto them, It is written,*
> *My house is the house of prayer: but ye*
> *have made it a den of thieves.*
> *(Luke 19:45–46)*

The above Scripture passage shows Jesus starting the week by visiting the temple. Jesus knows the sufferings that He must soon face, so He goes to the house of prayer. When He arrives at the temple during the week of Passover, the people are doing disturbing things. Jesus Christ found overpricing of sacrificial animals and exchanging of currency. Jesus announced, "It is written, My house is the house of prayer..." (verse 46), and then proceeded to clear out the place! This same act of merchandising in the temple is recorded in John 2:13–16.

Have you ever been disturbed about the things that were going on in your house? Instead of getting discouraged, cast out the corruption in the Name of Jesus and get ready for glory!

Day Two

> *And it came to pass, that on*
> *one of those days, as he taught*
> *the people in the temple,*
> *and preached the gospel,*
> *the chief priests and the scribes*
> *came upon him with the elders,*
>
> *And spake unto him, saying,*
> *Tell us, by what authority doest thou*
> *these things? or who is he*
> *that gave thee this authority?*
> *(Luke 20:1–2)*

The chief priests, scribes, and elders challenged Jesus' authority; however, He refused to be intimidated. Christ understood His position in the Kingdom and the source of His authority. Like Christ, to hold on for the glory, we must clearly understand our place in the plan of God.

Has anyone ever challenged your authority? Has the sincerity of your motive ever been questioned? As you wait for God's glory to be manifested in your life, religious bullies might tell you, "Well, who are you and who gave you that right? Jesus' authority was challenged and yours will be too. Let's continue reading Luke, chapter 20, verses 3–8:

And he answered and said unto them,
I will also ask you one thing,
and answer me:

The baptism of John, was it from heaven,
or of men?

And they reasoned with themselves,
saying, If we shall say, From heaven; he
will say, Why then believed ye him not?

But and if we say, Of men; all the people
will stone us: for they be persuaded that
John was a prophet.

And they answered, that they
could not tell whence it was.

And Jesus said unto them,
Neither tell I you by what authority
I do these things.

Here Jesus continues His dialogue with the Jewish leaders. They had come together to confront the authority by which He was operating when He threw the moneychangers out of the temple. Jesus responded to their questions by asking a question. They did not answer Jesus' question; therefore He refused to answer theirs. Sometimes we must choose not to enter into a debate or discussion with people whose purpose is to challenge or discredit our faith. We must simply respond by saying; "Just keep watching me because I am *destined for glory*."

Day Three

> *Now the feast of unleavened bread*
> *drew nigh, which is called the Passover.*
>
> *And the chief priests and scribes*
> *sought how they might kill him;*
> *for they feared the people.*
>
> *Then entered Satan into Judas*
> *surnamed Iscariot, being of the*
> *number of the twelve.*
>
> *And he went his way, and communed*
> *with the chief priests and captains,*
> *how he might betray him unto them.*
>
> *And they were glad, and covenanted to*
> *give him money.*
>
> *And he promised, and sought*
> *opportunity to betray him*
> *unto them in the absence*
> *of the multitude.*
> *(Luke 22:1–6)*

On day three the chief priests and scribes conspired to kill Jesus during the Passion Week. Someone from Jesus' inner circle, one of the twelve disciples who served as the treasurer, approached these leaders and essentially said, "Do you want Him? I'll give Him to you."

When we consider what happened to Jesus, we must look at how it applies to Christians today. Being betrayed by people who are close to us is terrible. A friend betraying a friend is as painful as a festering sore. Whether the pain is emotional or physical, both are very intense. I have seen many people wounded for years because someone who was their friend betrayed them.

There are individuals in churches all over the world who have stumbled because someone they confided in and depended upon told the enemy, "I'll get them for you." However, we must stay encouraged and not be deterred from our ultimate goal of glorifying God.

Betrayal is not strong enough to stop destiny. Our responsibility is to keep our minds and hearts focused on obtaining His glory. I often talk to people who are disturbed and ready to leave the church, due to betrayal. Many question God: "How did You let this happen to me? I do not want to go to church and I do not want to be saved anymore. There is no one I can trust." These immobilizing thoughts and feelings are common when a person experiences betrayal.

The writer of Hebrews admonishes us in chapter 12, verse 2, to look unto Jesus, the author and finisher of our faith; who for the joy that was set before Him endured the cross, despised the shame, then set down at the right hand of the throne of God. We must keep our attention focused on Jesus, our supreme example of perseverance. Don't ever let anyone's behavior control your mind and stop you from pursuing what God has purposed for you.

Day Four

Jesus is getting close not only to Calvary's Cross, He's getting closer to the manifested glory that God pre-ordained to be revealed through Him. But before He gets to the glory, everything around Him gets worse. Let's read Luke 22:21–24:

> *But, behold, the hand of him*
> *that betrayeth me*
> *is with me on the table.*
>
> *And truly the Son of man goeth,*
> *as it was determined: but woe*
> *unto that man by whom he is betrayed!*
>
> *And they began to inquire among*
> *themselves, which of them it was*
> *that should do this thing.*
>
> *And there was also a strife among them,*
> *which of them should be*
> *accounted the greatest.*

Here, Jesus is eating His last Passover meal with His twelve disciples, one of whom is the man who leads Him to His death. Jesus did not confront or say anything malicious to His betrayer. He simply said, "Woe unto that man." After hearing this disquieting statement, the next verse says that the disciples "began to inquire among themselves."

Not only is Jesus dealing with a man planning to betray Him, His disciples are starting to whisper about who the traitor is. To add insult to injury, they get into a heated discussion about who among them is the greatest. At a time when Jesus needs someone helping Him, these disciples are fussing about who will be the next one in charge (Luke 22:24)! Sometimes when you need your friends to support and pray for you, it might be the furthest thing from their minds.

When we suffer tremendous affliction, focusing on the promise that is on the other side helps us to get through. Approaching adversity with the attitude of making it through one day at a time makes the journey much easier. This is the reason I am showing you, day by day, the events leading to Jesus' death on Calvary's Cross. Jesus superbly illustrates how to handle heart-breaking experiences, rejection, and betrayal.

Our Lord operated with a divine and human nature. At this point, things got so bad that He literally did not want to continue. Have you ever had a situation that was so bad you did not want to go on? Has the pressure ever been so hard and heavy you just wanted to say, "Forget it?" Well, do not let the devil beat you up about it because even if you wanted to say, "Forget it," as long as you endure, everything will be all right. Jesus, in the human almost said, "Forget it," but His desire to do the will of His Father prevailed.

Luke, chapter 22, describes the passion of Jesus, beginning with His agony in the garden of Gethsemane and continuing to His death on the cross at a place called Golgotha (Matthew 27:33, Mark 15:22, John 19:17). Because of His sorrow, Jesus needed someone to help pray and lift Him up. Instead, His disciples were arguing and posturing for leadership roles. Just imagine; this is the toughest time of His life and He could not even depend on those closest to Him for spiritual support.

Jesus and His eleven disciples (Judas Iscariot was not present at this time; he was busy planning to betray Jesus) went to the Mount of Olives, a quiet and peaceful place. Everyone should have a specific place of serenity where he or she can go to 'get away from it all'. For Jesus and His disciples this place of rest was the Garden of Gethsemane. Even though all of Jesus' disciples went to the Mount of Olives, He instructed some of them to remain behind. There are times in our lives, while on this road to destiny, that we must separate from those who are close to us as we continue fulfilling God's plan.

Jesus Christ allowed Peter, James, and John to continue with Him a little farther in the garden, then asked them to stay back and watch. Some roads to destiny are narrow ones in that they are only meant for you, the individual to travel. There are times when no one can walk along side of you, not your mother, father, spouse, best friend, not even your prayer partner—it will be just you and the LORD. The time will come when you must walk to your own destiny. Jesus walked a little farther in the garden—but alone—this time to kneel down and pray.

He prayed, "Father, if thou be willing, remove this cup from me." Jesus knew where He had to go. He knew what was before Him. Jesus knew that the hour had come, the hour in which He would be offered as a sacrificial Lamb of God and drink of the bitter cup of death. Jesus knew He had to suffer these things before entering into His glory.

Nevertheless

Although the entire week had been tough, Jesus said, "Nevertheless." *My disciples were supposed to be My prayer warriors. I needed them to walk, watch and pray with Me.* "Nevertheless." *A chosen one of My disciples with whom I supped has betrayed Me.* "Nevertheless." *I've only tried to do good by helping those in need.* "Nevertheless, not My will, but Thine be done."

As Jesus prayed to His Heavenly Father, He totally released His will to do that of the One who sent Him. At such a grim time as this, Jesus was weak and sorrowful. In the *Amplified Bible*, Matthew 26:38a says, "Then He said to them, my soul is very sad and deeply grieved, so that I am almost dying of sorrow." Even though it seemed as if Jesus was totally alone—God was there! He heard and answered His Son's prayer. God sent one of His messengers, an angel, to strengthen Jesus in His weakness. Thank God for ministering angels who strengthen and encourage us during our most difficult moments.

This is why it is important to remember, far above the pain and heartache, that we are *destined for glory*. When we don't know what to say and the only thing we have to offer is tears, God will send an angel to comfort us. He gives them charge over us to protect, defend, and preserve us on our path to destiny (Psalm 91:11). Our Heavenly Father will take us from glory to glory!

Luke 22:44 says, "And being in an agony he prayed more earnestly: and his sweat was as it were great drops of blood falling down to the ground." Jesus then got up and went to His disciples whom He found asleep from grief and sorrow (verse 45). Peter, James, and John could not bear the stress any longer. They said, "We can't take it. You are the great master and teacher. You are the prophet. You are the pastor, not us!"

Day Five

And Peter said, Man,
I know not what thou sayest.
And immediately, while he
yet spake, the cock crew.

And the Lord turned,
and looked upon Peter.
And Peter remembered
the word of the Lord,
how he had said unto him,
Before the cock crow,
thou shalt deny me thrice.

And Peter went out,
and wept bitterly.
(Luke 22:60–62).

This is Friday. Peter had been with Jesus from the beginning of His ministry. Simon Peter was one of the first men chosen to be Jesus' disciple (Matthew 4:18). Jesus had been to Peter's house and prayed for his mother-in-law. Our Lord was with Peter, who was a fisherman by trade, when he had fished all night long but hadn't caught anything. Jesus gave Peter instructions on how to increase his "fishing business," resulting in a catch that was so large that Peter had to call for help to bring it in. Jesus had helped Peter time and time again, but when Jesus needs Peter the most, that same man said, "I don't even know Him." Have you ever had any Fridays in your life, days full of rejection and denial? Let's continue reading. Luke 23:21 says:

> *But they cried, saying,*
> *Crucify him, crucify him.*

Have you ever felt like people were trying to crucify you? Do you have enemies who want you "out of the picture?" Are there people who want to dig your grave even though you haven't done anything to them? If so, you may know how Jesus must have felt.

Not Guilty

> *And he said unto them the third time,*
> *Why, what evil hath he done? I have found*
> *no cause of death in him: I will therefore*
> *chastise him, and let him go.*
> *(Luke 23:22)*

Jesus was brought before Pontius Pilate, the governor of Judea. He was brought before Pilate because of His alleged criminal actions. Pilate disagreed with the people's verdict. He did not consider Jesus to be guilty of any crime that warranted the death penalty. Pilate asked the crowd three times what evil Jesus had done? He wanted to know why they demanded that this man's life be taken. He told the crowd, "I have found no cause of death in him." Then he made a suggestion, "Chastise Him and let Him go" (verse 22).

However, the crowd protested. Present at the sentencing with Jesus was a criminal who was guilty of murder. Those who had gathered wanted Pilate to release the guilty man. As for Jesus, they wanted Him put to death. Pilate gave in to their demands and Jesus began walking the path to Calvary to be crucified, even though Pilate found Him *not guilty*.

Mockery

When we experience injustice, loneliness, and betrayal, we can look at what Jesus did, and know how to handle it. The people gawked, gazed, and cast lots to divide His garments. The rulers made sarcastic remarks: "You saved others; if you are 'all that', then save yourself!" The soldiers mocked Him too, offering vinegar and saying, "This Is The King Of The Jews" (Luke 23:38).

Just as Jesus' accusers, sometimes people will look at an individual going through problems and say, "Uh-huh; I knew he wouldn't amount to anything." I discovered that everyone in church is not happy for us when we are on our way to a blessing. Everyone is not pleased when we glorify God. But we cannot allow this to stop us from pursuing our destiny. It is not our fault these people have a problem. However, we must be prepared for attacks and know what to do when they happen.

Everybody in church is not saved. Don't be surprised if the news of an embarrassing situation spreads like wildfire. When your church enemies hear that your child is in trouble, don't be surprised if they talk about you and your troubled child. It wasn't unbelievers or sinners that mocked and denied Jesus. It was the religious leaders and church folks!

Just a Step Away

The crowd was oblivious to the fact that Jesus was just a step away from glory (the splendor and majesty of God being revealed through Him). When someone challenges your authority and tries to crucify you, don't worry because you are just a step away from glory. Jesus suffered a level of ridicule and humiliation that most of us will not even come close to experiencing. The onlookers were making a party of His plight while they gambled over His raiment and mocked Him. People will have a "party" and talk about you too. They will drink soda pop and eat chicken wings and potato chips with dip and have a good time. But you must stay focused as you persevere in your time of suffering because God's will is just a step away.

Remember Me

*And one of the malefactors which were
hanged railed on him, saying,
If thou be Christ, save thyself and us.*

*But the other answering rebuked him,
saying, Dost not thou fear God,
seeing thou art
in the same condemnation?*

*And we indeed justly; for we receive the
due reward of our deeds: but this man
hath done nothing amiss.*

*And he said unto Jesus, Lord,
remember me when thou comest
into thy kingdom.*

*And Jesus said unto him,
Verily I say unto thee,
To day shalt thou be with me in paradise.*
(Luke 23:39–43)

This is a great lesson on humility. Two criminals were crucified on Calvary with Jesus: one on His left and the other on His right. One of the criminals joined the crowd in condemning Jesus. However, the other acknowledged his own guilt. Even though he knew he deserved to be punished, this man looked at Jesus and said, "Remember me." All of us deserve terrible punishment, but I believe that many of us, like the repentant criminal, have looked to God and pleaded, "Remember me."

Let Go and Let God

And when Jesus had cried with
a loud voice, he said, Father, into thy
hands I commend my spirit: and having
said thus, he gave up the ghost.
(Luke 23:46)

Sometimes, God is just waiting for us to give up our will. I'm not talking about quitting. I mean give up and tell Him, "This is not my battle—it's Yours. I release my will. God, You handle it because I can't. I'm just going to stand here and watch You make a way and bring me out."

In Jesus' darkest hour, His final act was to totally relinquish His spirit into the hands of His Father. We need to do likewise in our darkest hours. *Let go and let God.* He will provide whatever you need to hold on until the glory comes.

Sunday Is on the Way

Now upon the first day of the week, very
early in the morning, they came unto the
sepulchre, bringing the spices which they
had prepared, and certain others with them.

And they found the stone rolled away
from the sepulchre.

And they entered in, and found not the
body of the Lord Jesus.
(Luke 24:1–3)

80

Jesus died! They took Him down from the cross, laid Him in a tomb, and sealed it with a great stone. His disciples and followers thought this was the end. They failed to realize that Sunday was on the way (Matthew 28:1, Luke 24:1, *The Living Bible*). We cannot stop because we are denied and rejected by those closest to us, nor can we give up because of injustices. We cannot even quit because it is so dark and gloomy. We must spiritually move over into Sunday, because on Sunday the glory is revealed.

Glory! He Is Risen!

The finality of Jesus' death became a stinging reality, as His body was placed in the sepulchre. His followers felt totally defeated. Friday and Saturday have passed and it is now Sunday morning. When Mary Magdalene, Joanna, Mary (the mother of James), and other women went to anoint Jesus' body, they could not find Him (Luke 24:10). He had risen just as He said. The two angels had to remind the women that Jesus held true to His Word, predicting His death, burial, and resurrection. Jesus had risen from all gloom, despair, and embarrassment with all power given unto Him in Heaven and earth (Matthew 28:18).

I declare unto you, by the Word of God and by the power of the Holy Spirit, that those of us who are faithful and true followers of the Lord Jesus Christ are *destined for glory*. There might be days, situations, and seasons of darkness, but we must hold fast to the promises before us. We must be determined to keep smiling and to assure one another that God is true to His Word. Sunday is coming! Expect the glory of the Lord to come forth in your life and move in your favor.

Positioned for Glory

And I, brethren, when I came to you, came not with excellency of speech or of wisdom, declaring unto you the testimony of God.

Which none of the princes of this world knew: for had they known it, they would not have crucified the Lord of glory.
(1 Corinthians 2:1, 8)

Please allow me to reiterate a very important point from chapter four. If Jesus' opponents had known the truth of His identity, they would have left Him alone. Had the enemy known that the Calvary cross experience would bring salvation to mankind and expand the Kingdom of God, he truly would have left Jesus Christ alone! His attacks are part of our training for the greatest hour of our lives.

The only thing the devil can do to committed believers is get us positioned for glory. Jesus fulfilled God's purpose and plan for His life, and we will too. We can do all things through Christ who strengthens us (Philippians 4:13). Be determined to keep moving forward in destiny until the journey is completed. It's not over until God says it's over. In the meantime, let me teach you more about the glory.

SIX

DECLARE HIS GLORY!

lory is a term most of us have heard someone shout out during religious services and events, especially when the praise is high. It is a word—with spiritual connotations—that flows deep in the believer's spirit. During times of passionate prayer, intimate worship, or during a soul-stirring song, this word can burst forth and ignite the atmosphere. Many churches have experienced individuals in the congregation known for praising the Lord by shouting the word, "Glory!"

Believers should not use this word idly, nor should we underestimate the significance of proclaiming the glory of God. *Glory* is the Word and power of God manifested in the physical realm. When we declare "glory," we are acknowledging the magnificence, majesty, and excellence of the Most High God. The miracle working power, wealth, and abundance—even the richness of God are in His glory.

My goal in this chapter is to help you understand your God-given authority to declare His glory, in the Name of Jesus Christ, in every area of your life. Many Christians spend too much time trying to give the impression that the devil has never had them against the ropes in the boxing ring of life. Being saved and filled with the Holy Spirit does not stop the enemy from trying to knock us around every once in a while. Instead of pretending, we need to rise up on our "Holy Ghost tippy-toes" and declare God's glory. When the devil is trying to wreck your home, family, and health, stand-up and say, "I declare glory!" When that malicious, evil, backstabbing devil shows up in your situation don't hesitate or hold back—*Stand tall and declare God's glory!*

We Must Know Him

Individuals do not have to be "saved" to see God's glory. The Bible says, "The heavens declare his righteousness, and all the people see his glory" (Psalm 97:6). Anything that is glorious stands out. Glory draws attention and people, saved and unsaved, are attracted to it. Unbelievers might not recognize God's glory when they see it; however, these individuals will sense that they have witnessed something that cannot be explained in the natural. The glory of God is supernatural! It is majestic, splendorous, brilliant, and radiant.

Though the whole world may *see* His glory, *declaring* it is entirely different. People who declare His glory must know Him. You must know His Word and His ways because there will surely come a time when you will need the manifested power of God operating in your life. When the enemy comes in like a flood, declare God's glory. Surely, the Spirit of the LORD will lift up a standard against him (Isaiah 59:19). God will step in and keep you on course to your place of destiny.

Let me warn you—this word is not for "baby believers." To operate at this level takes mature faith and being in right relationship with God. When believers declare His glory, we are announcing that no matter what the enemy is trying to do, we take authority over him in the Name of Jesus Christ. We are confessing that the will and purpose of God shall be manifested in every area of our lives right here and now!

Please do not misunderstand me; this is not about taking on the enemy in your own strength. Declaring glory is about knowing that because of Jesus Christ, you have the victory in every situation. You must get to the point at which your trust in the LORD's Word is complete, so that the moment satan tries to wreak havoc in your life, you will warn him, "Stop right there in the Name of Jesus Christ!" When God's Word has been planted deeply in your spirit, you'll have the confidence to get in the devil's face and shout, "You cannot have my marriage, children, or money because I *declare His glory!*"

The 102nd Psalm

I want to take you to the 102nd Psalm as a foundational text and go deeper into this word concerning God's glory. Let's begin at verse 13:

Thou shalt arise, and have mercy
upon Zion: for the time to favour her,
*yea, the **set time**, is come.*

For thy servants take pleasure in her
stones, and favour the dust thereof.

So the heathen shall fear the name
of the LORD, and all the kings
of the earth thy glory.

When the LORD shall build up Zion,
*he shall appear in his **glory**.*
(vv. 13–16)

The 102nd Psalm is often referred to as a "prayer of affliction." Biblical scholars have different opinions as to the identity of the writer of this psalm. We do know from the language used that the writer, while in the spirit, saw the LORD's plan to restore His people to a position of dignity and honor. The psalmist speaks of a *set time* when the people of God will no longer be downcast; for His favor shall be poured out on us. He shares with us, "The time to favour her [God's people] has come, yea, the set time, is come." He continues by saying that when the nations and people who worship other gods see how magnificently and powerfully God restores His people, they will fear and reverence Him. Even the heathen and the kings of the earth will honor the LORD, when He appears in His glory.

Writing this prophecy would be impossible for some-one who never spent meaningful time with God. The writer undoubtedly had an intimate relationship with the LORD and was sensitive to His purpose and plans. We can also infer from the tenacity and the boldness of the language used that the writer had strong faith and was confident that God would show compassion and grace toward His people. In this chapter, we will examine three Bible personalities: David, Daniel, and Nehemiah because any one of these three men could have certainly been the writer of this 102nd Psalm.

David—A Man after God's Own Heart

Many scholars believe that King David is the most likely person to have written the 102nd Psalm. Most Christians who have knowledge of the Bible realize something about this man of valor who lived his life *pursuing the heart of God.* When he slew Goliath, the champion of the Philistines, David became a hero in the land of Judah. All Israel feared Goliath. Goliath was not only a giant; he was an ugly giant! If his size didn't frighten you, his appearance would "ugly" you to your knees. He was a fearful looking terror.

David accomplished great feats and held many impressive positions during his lifetime including musician (harpist), valiant warrior, and king. However, one of the most important things that can be said about David is that he was *anointed.* Before he ever faced Goliath, David had an anointing. In other words, he was divinely appointed and equipped to fulfill God's purpose and plan for his life. When God gives someone an assignment that places him face to face with the adversary, that person needs supernatural power from above. The individual needs to know beyond all doubt that God has called him, for such a time as this. I like to put it this way: *the anointing takes you to your destiny.*

There are many qualities about Psalm 102 that lead one to conclude that David is the author. The writer begins his appeal to the LORD by talking about his affliction, but shortly after, he declares the glory of God. During times of trouble, it was characteristic of David to cry out to God; but David would always recall how God had delivered him time and time again. David knew about the awesome and incomparable power of God from personal experience. Let's take a closer look at David's encounter with Goliath as described in 1 Samuel, chapter 17.

Who Is this Uncircumcised Philistine?

The chapter begins with the Israelites at war with the Philistines. David was taking food to his three brothers who were in King Saul's army, when Goliath challenged them. When the men of Israel saw Goliath, they were "scared-to-death" and ran. The giant Philistine walked around daring any soldier to come and fight him. In his challenge, he added that if any man killed him, then the Philistines would be their servants.

When young David heard all this talk about Goliath, he stepped forward and said, *"Who is this uncircumcised Philistine, that he should defy the armies of the living God?"* (1 Samuel 17:26). Goliath did not intimidate David because he understood that nothing was too hard for the LORD, his God!

When King Saul heard that David wanted to fight Goliath, he told David, in essence, *"Okay. If you want to go and fight Goliath, go and the LORD be with you"* (1 Samuel 17:37). Saul's men began to dress David in the king's armor. Keep in mind that David was a man of small stature. When Saul's men placed all that heavy equipment on David, he basically told them, "Wait a minute! I didn't have all this on the last time God helped me. You did not dress me then. As a matter of fact, none of you were there. A lion and a bear came to attack my father's sheep, but the LORD helped me to kill them. The same God that delivered me before will deliver me again!"

David got his slingshot and selected five smooth stones. He didn't choose five because he doubted God. David was confident he could kill Goliath with one shot. But, just in case Goliath's brothers showed up, David had something for them too!

God needs individuals like David who will stand strong and ask without fear, "What is this trouble? What is this problem to the God I serve?" The Bible says, "...but the people that do know their God shall be strong, and do exploits" (Daniel 11:32). Knowing God in a personal and intimate way teaches the believer about the faithfulness of God. We are living in a time when the believers need to be courageous and know that with God they will get the victory every time. David knew his God, and was successful in slaying Goliath, the giant Philistine.

David Holds His Peace

As David's popularity grew, Saul became extremely jealous. So jealous, in fact, that Saul attempted to kill him on at least four occasions. The Bible tells us that David had the opportunity to kill Saul more than once, but he said, in effect, "I will hold my peace." He was a man of integrity and understood that the fight belonged to God. In 1 Chronicles 16:22, this man of valor wrote, "Touch not mine anointed, and do my prophets no harm." He was able to maintain respect and honor for Saul, even though he knew Saul wanted to kill him.

Given David's history and personality, many scholars and theologians believe he was the author of the 102nd Psalm. Others believe another great man of the Bible wrote this Psalm. Let's look at another Old Testament writer, visionary leader, and great man of faith. Go with me to the Book of Daniel.

Daniel—A Man of Excellence

For many years, godly prophets gave messages, warning the children of Israel of the soon-to-come judgment against them because of their rebellion and idol worship. They were admonished time and time again that because of their unrepentant ways, God would allow their enemies to take them into captivity. Well it happened! The Book of Daniel opens with a discussion of the Babylonian captivity, whereby Judah was seized (Daniel 1:1–2). King Nebuchadnezzar took Daniel and three other children of Judah (verse 6) who exhibited exceptional intellectual abilities and talents and held them captive in Babylon. The Word of God says that Daniel was graced with "knowledge and skill in all learning and wisdom" and also "understanding in all visions and dreams" (Daniel 1:17).

Babylon was a country that served idols and strange gods. After King Nebuchadnezzar discovered Daniel's brilliance, he began to promote the young man. While serving under King Nebuchadnezzar, Daniel could have easily fallen into the practices of the Babylonians. However, he purposed in his heart that he would not defile himself. Daniel was determined to remain committed to the true and living God.

King Nebuchadnezzar was very fond of Daniel, as was his son, King Belshazzar, who ascended to the throne after him. King Belshazzar was later slain, and King Darius came into power. The Bible says that King Darius saw an *excellent* spirit in Daniel (Daniel 6:3). The new king set up his administration with 120 princes to rule over the entire kingdom. The 120 princes reported to three presidents, of whom Daniel was the number one man. Because of Daniel's excellent spirit, he was highly favored in the king's court. If King Darius could have had his way, he would have set Daniel over the whole realm!

Chapter 6 of the Book of Daniel describes how the presidents and princes were jealous of Daniel. They came together to determine what they could use against him, but they found no weakness. Daniel 6:4b says, "Forasmuch as he was faithful, neither was there any error or fault found in him."

The presidents and princes concluded that the only thing they could use to destroy Daniel was his relationship and obedience to the God of his fathers. Daniel's enemies came up with a plan to convince the king to sign a 30-day decree forbidding anyone to pray to any god other than King Darius. Anyone who prayed to a god other than King Darius within this period of time would be thrown into the lions' den.

They convinced King Darius that this was a good idea, and he established a decree prohibiting prayer to any god or man other than himself for one month. After the king signed the order, the Bible lets us know that Daniel continued his daily prayer schedule. He prayed three times a day, giving thanks to his God (Daniel 6:10).

Some, possibly the majority, of believers would have closed their windows and sneaked around the corner to pray. Yet, Daniel did not let the threat of death stop him from praying to his God in the same manner. He went into his house and his windows were open. Daniel trusted the LORD.

Your God Will Deliver!

Of course, the men who came up with the idea about the decree immediately told King Darius that Daniel had prayed to his God. They reminded the king: "This decree has been signed and cannot be changed. There are witnesses who saw Daniel pray to his God. Therefore, he must be thrown in the lions' den."

When the king realized how his decree was used to destroy Daniel, he was distraught. He tried, but could not come up with a way to get around the decree and had no choice but to order his men to throw Daniel into that den. But he knew something about the faithfulness of Daniel's God. He told Daniel, "Thy God whom thou servest continually, he will deliver thee" (Daniel 6:16).

Daniel 6:18 states that the king could not sleep and spent the entire night fasting. He arose early the next morning, hoping that no harm had come to his beloved friend. When the king came to the den, he cried out, "O, Daniel, servant of the living God, is thy God, whom thou servest continually, able to deliver thee from the lions?" (Daniel 6:20). Then he heard Daniel proclaim, "O king, live forever" (verse 21).

Daniel told the king that God had sent an angel who shut the lions' mouths (Daniel 6:22). In other words, God sent manifestation of His magnificent and radiant power to the lions' den and delivered Daniel. King Darius instructed his men to bring Daniel out of that den. Daniel 6:23 says, "So Daniel was taken up out of the den, and no manner of hurt was found upon him, because he believed in his God." As a result of Daniel's deliverance, King Darius made a decree for all the people throughout his kingdom. He declared that men must tremble and fear before the true and living God of Daniel. This dangerous den experience brought reverence and honor to God from a heathen nation (Psalm 102:14). Daniel was delivered and God got glory. If you ever find yourself in the den of danger remember that our God is a deliverer. He will send His glory to deliver you too!

Do you know what happened to Daniel's enemies? When Daniel was pulled out of the lions' den, his enemies were thrown into it! King Darius also had their children and their wives thrown in as well. When we trust the LORD, He always handles our troubles. Daniel knew that God would take care of his enemies. Those lions had a good buffet dinner!

So, we have seen why some scholars believe David wrote Psalm 102 and why others believe it could have been Daniel. Certainly the confidence, courage, and boldness of Daniel make him a leading candidate. But there is at least one other person who could have written the 102nd Psalm. Let's go to the Book of Nehemiah.

Nehemiah—A Man on a Mission

Nehemiah, like Daniel, was taken captive at a young age and served under the authority of a heathen king. Nehemiah was graced with God's favor and held a prominent position in the Persian King Artaxerxes' court. This young lad from Judah was the king's cup-bearer (Nehemiah 1:11). Idolatry and paganism surrounded Nehemiah, yet he remained faithful to his God. Nehemiah was determined to walk in his destiny and fulfill his God-ordained purpose.

Chapter 1 begins with Nehemiah asking his Jewish brethren about the condition of those who had escaped the Babylonian captivity and returned to Jerusalem. When Nehemiah heard that the walls around Jerusalem were broken down and the gates were burned with fire, he wept and mourned for several days (verses 3–4). I believe that during his time of fasting and praying (verse 4), he determined in his mind to do the work of the LORD. Nehemiah must have thought, *My father's place has no business looking like that. God is too great for His city, the city of my forefathers, to be in disarray. I cannot sit back and do nothing while my fathers' sepulchers lie waste and the gates are consumed with fire.*

In Nehemiah, chapter 2, we find him serving wine to King Artaxerxes. The king noticed the countenance on Nehemiah's face and asked him, in essence, "Why the sad look?" Nehemiah told the ruler that he was sad because Jerusalem was in ruins. He asked Nehemiah what was his request. After praying and seeking the will of God, Nehemiah asked King Artaxerxes for permission to go to Jerusalem and rebuild the city walls of his ancestors (Nehemiah 2:5).

Let me help you grasp what Nehemiah was embarking upon. Many years prior, Ezra had taken several thousand men back to Jerusalem to rebuild the walls and the Temple. According to Ezra 6:13–17, with the leadership of Zerubbabel, Ezra was able to successfully complete the Temple. However, due to fierce opposition, he was not able to finish the work of the walls. The enemy attacked Ezra and his men so fiercely that they had to quit. King Artaxerxes told Ezra, in effect, "Just leave it alone. Stop the work immediately" (Ezra 4:17–24).

So, for several years the walls laid in ruin. Then came Nehemiah, *a man on a mission.* Nehemiah said in his heart, *I don't care who tried it before. I don't care who has been there and had to leave. I'm going to rebuild the city of my fathers.*

Try Again

Have you ever wanted to do something and someone told you, "Well you know, they tried that before and it didn't work." Nehemiah did not let that kind of talk stop him from accomplishing what he set out to do for the LORD. Nehemiah knew that he, too, would face great opposition so he prayed asking God to strengthen his hands. God answered his prayers, allowing the walls of Jerusalem to be built in fifty-two days (Nehemiah 6:15). Sanballat, Tobiah, and Geshem tried to distract and discourage Nehemiah but to no avail. Even his enemies realized that this work had been done with divine help (Nehemiah 6:16). Through the organization, planning, and determination of Nehemiah, the will of God was manifested.

Whether the writer of the 102nd Psalm was David, Daniel, or Nehemiah, they were all great men of faith who knew and trusted God. The body of Christ can learn much from these valiant men of God who determined in their heart that no matter how negative the situation looked, they were going to stand strong, and *declare His glory.* They refused to run away and give up due to opposition.

Believers who are *destined for glory* cannot afford to be passive and nervous. When the enemy stirs up trouble, don't give up. Be strong in the LORD and in the power of His might (Ephesians 6:10). Understand that God will fight our battles. Just stand still and see the salvation of the LORD. And when you see His salvation, you will see His glory!

Delayed, but not Denied

We must get to a place of spiritual maturity where we understand that our deliverance may be delayed, but it's never denied. Believers whose faith has matured have experienced the hand of God moving on their behalf time and time again. This level of trusting God does not develop without having trouble. These believers made it not because the enemy and his "imps" chose to ignore them, but because they were willing to stand firm and say, "I will not wimp out. I am not afraid of the enemy's assaults against me." As stated in chapter two of this book, God has a set time already appointed for our deliverance. Therefore, we realize that victory although delayed, is definitely not denied.

Call on Jesus

The adversary wants to intimidate God's people. He wants us to think we do not know what to say, and sometimes we don't. The enemy will try to make us feel like we do not know what to do, and many times we don't. But when you know how to call on Jesus, you can walk into any situation and declare God's glory. You can walk into your home and in your child's school and declare glory. You can go into the bank *declaring His glory!*

There is unlimited power and authority in the Name of Jesus Christ, which enables us to change any condition or situation by speaking those things that be not as though they were (Romans 4:17).

If there is doubt and hesitancy in your mind about God's ability to take over any situation, then don't even think about declaring His glory. Faith and fear do not mix. They are in total opposition, and cannot operate together. It takes faith in God and His Word to declare glory. Nehemiah responded the same as Daniel. You can too, when times get lean and situations get really rough, just remember Daniel who *believed* in his God (Daniel 6:23). God did not prevent the tossing of Daniel into the lions' den, but He certainly made sure that Daniel got out!

But Thou, O LORD

My days are like a shadow that declineth;
and I am withered like grass.

But thou, O LORD, shalt endure
for ever; and thy remembrance
unto all generations.
(Psalm 102:11–12)

In the above passages from the 102nd Psalm the writer laments, "My days are like a shadow that declineth, and I am withered like grass." The psalmist is looking at himself and his life and cries out that he is dying. Then he says, in effect, "Wait a minute. Why should I look at myself when I can enter into His glory and experience His power to transform and transcend my present situation?"

Sometimes when we're feeling overwhelmed with the cares of life, we need to just look up and say, "But thou, O LORD." The next time the enemy shows up with a problem, lift your hands and say, "But thou, O LORD." When pain hits your body or your child is misbehaving, just say, "But thou, O LORD!" Whatever it is that you need, seek the One who endures forever and whose compassion reaches all generations.

He will regard the prayer of the destitute,
and not despise their prayer.
(Psalm 102:17)

You may be experiencing lack in your life, but never hesitate to call on the Name of the LORD. He waits attentively and His ears are open to your prayers. God hears your prayers and His glory is going to appear and take care of the lack. Scripture declares that He regards the prayer of the destitute and never despises their petitions.

Raise Your Expectations

The writer of the 102nd Psalm was speaking to a future generation. I believe *we are that generation* which God has chosen for His glory. We must never minimize what God has planned for us. Now is the time for the body of Christ to come to the place where we expect the Word of God to manifest and for His glory to be revealed in its fullness.

Today, many Christians have fallen into a lull where they think that the LORD is not healing, delivering, or prospering His people. We must come out of the mind-set of a "little" God and get back on track to where we understand that He is the God of "more than enough!" I can hear the LORD saying, "My people are not expecting much. I want to do so much more." God is looking for people who will not hesitate to say, "I don't want to ask for less than what You have planned for me. I pray that every area of my life flourishes *according to Your Word,* and that the power of Your glory continually operate on my behalf."

His glory is going to rise to the level of our expectations. When we live in expectation of what God will do, our minds are open to Him. We become submissive to

His will, wanting only what He wants for us. The LORD can impregnate us with vision, stimulate our imagination, and motivate our hands to work. Excitement will begin to churn in our spirit as God guides our footsteps. He is your Heavenly Father so never hesitate to ask Him, "Which way do You want me to go LORD?" I know that I am not going to be in the same place, this time next year or even next week. Your Spirit is maturing in my life. I don't know how You are going to do it, but I know in my spirit that Your glory is being revealed in me!"

Thine Expectation Shall Not Be Cut Off

What are you expecting from the LORD? Expect Him to raise you up, move you forward, and promote you to higher levels. Don't let the enemy intimidate your mind. Some people can praise God with strong faith on Sunday and shout Hallelujah on Wednesday. Then something may happen on Thursday that makes it difficult for them to praise, and they begin to question God's plan for their lives. The devil will attempt to make you doubt God and then step back to watch your reaction. He wants to prove that you are not serious about fulfilling your destiny. This is the time when you need to remember Proverbs 23:18, which says:

> *For surely there is an end; and thine*
> *expectation shall not be cut off.*

We cannot allow the enemy to destroy, dilute, or drown our expectation. The favor of the LORD will come, not because of who you are, or who I am; His favor will come simply because we have positioned ourselves in His will, and our motives and mindsets are in rightstanding before Him. *Declare His Glory* and it shall be revealed in your life!

Chapter seven takes a look at another aspect of our destiny—the transformation of the believer into the glorious image of our Lord and Savior, Jesus Christ. It's time for the body of Christ to know and do what it takes to be more like Him. Although there might be detours on the way, I assure you that you will never regret taking God's path to your destiny.

SEVEN

FROM GLORY
TO GLORY

But we all, with open face beholding
as in a glass the glory of the Lord,
are changed into the same image
from glory to glory,
even as by the Spirit of the Lord.
(2 Corinthians 3:18)

Reaching a level of spiritual maturity and refinement where God's glory manifests in the life of the believer is an ongoing process. We studied earlier how man was originally created in God's image and after His likeness (Genesis 1:26) for the purpose of reflecting His glory (Isaiah 43:7). When man disobeyed God's instruction, instead of reflecting His character and glory, man began to reflect sin, and a character contrary to that of God's. As a result, no longer reflecting our Creator's image, mankind had to be restored into His image and glory.

In John 17:22 *TLB,* Jesus said, as He prayed to His Heavenly Father; "I have given to them the glory and honor which You have given Me." It is our Lord's desire that the same glory we experience in Him should emanate from us. Romans 8:29 lets us know that we are *predestinated* to be conformed to the image of Jesus Christ. 2 Corinthians 3:18 says that we are changed *"from glory to glory"* into His image by the leading of the Holy Spirit. Jesus did the will of His Father, and the Father was glorified in Him. Ultimately, the body of Christ shall be glorified with Him (Romans 8:17, 30) and as glorified believers we will be one with our Lord and Savior as He establishes His Kingdom (Ephesians 1:10).

In this chapter, we will explore the transformation of the believer. Often, people want to take an elevator ride to the heights of glory, but God does not allow it. Most often we have to walk through each level, step by step. The road may not always be easy, but God's purpose and plan for the body of Christ shall come to pass. We shall become a reflection of God and all that He is to the praise of *His glory* (Ephesians 1:12)

Who Is Your Daddy?

If we truly claim God as our Father, we will exhibit His character and resemble Him in how we look, love, and live. Many have heard the old saying "Mama's baby, Daddy's maybe." There is seldom any question about a baby's mother, but the identity of the father can be a different story. When a baby is born, a father might look at the baby's features to find any resemblance which lets him know that the baby is his. As soon as the dad recognizes a familiar physical trait: "Yeah, that's my son! He has skinny legs and long toes just like me!" It's the same for the sons and daughters of God. There should never be any doubt that God is our Father because we should be a reflection of who He is.

Believers are part of God's royal family by adoption (Ephesians 1:5, Romans 8:15); therefore becoming Christ-like does not always come naturally. Though the Holy Spirit leads and guides us, we must also be educated and taught how to be more like Him. Fortunately, over a period of time, just as many adopted children begin to look and act like their adoptive parents, believers will experience a similar transformation. The mind of God will permeate our minds, and we will begin to express the thoughts of the Father and His glory.

The War in Our Flesh

The war in our flesh (James 4:1) is one of the major obstacles in the process to obtaining glory. If allowed, it could delay our fulfilling God's purpose and plan for our lives. Unfortunately, there are prominent people in the church today who are sending the wrong message about how to address the issue of carnal-minded believers. Some are teaching that believers should not be too hard on themselves when they fall into sin.

They teach that because of God's grace and mercy, the requirement for holy living is no longer relevant.

Yes, we must be thankful to God for His grace and mercy. Without them, none of us would have been able to attain any level of glory, let alone fulfill God's purpose and plan for our lives. Because of His grace and mercy, we are no longer crawling and stumbling like little babies learning to walk, but are developing into a body of believers who are mature in the faith. However, let me make this plain and clear: be careful not to slip into a lifestyle (repeated pattern) of falling down and getting up! Jude 24 *TLB* says, "And He is able to keep you from slipping and falling away, and to bring you, sinless and perfect, into His glorious presence with mighty shouts of everlasting joy."

The Spirit of the Lord is taking the body of Christ to a level where we must declare the unadulterated glory of God. As a young boy, I was taught that as soon as I made up my mind to live for Christ, the power and authority in the Word of God would help me live a life pleasing to Him. I am thankful that the teachings were not of a "diluted" gospel. Individuals who accept a weak doctrine often end up telling themselves, *God understands; I just can't help myself.*

Believers who thought this way often delayed or ruined their promotion to the next level of glory. Many fell down in sin when they should have been standing up in His righteousness, and found themselves improperly positioned for their blessing. The promises of God are always conditional. When someone truly knows what pleases the LORD, it is no longer acceptable to live *contrary* to His instructions. Let us embrace this word the psalmist wrote in Psalm 119:7–8 *TLB*, "After you have corrected me I will thank you by living as I should! I *will* obey! Oh, don't forsake me and let me slip back into sin again."

Words Have Power

I once heard someone make a statement that almost caused me to fall off my seat. They said, "We are all fornicators and idolaters." I said to myself, *That is a lie from the pit of hell, and I am sending it right back to the sender.* We must practice rejecting words, thoughts, and concepts that are contrary to God's written Word. Words are forceful enough to create as well as destroy. They can birth life or summon death. Words can build up or tear down. If someone calls himself a fornicator and idolater, eventually this is who he becomes. Believers must understand the creative power our words possess because of the indwelling of the Holy Spirit.

It is true that as long as we are in the "flesh" we will have a battle against sin. As stated previously in this chapter, there is a war in our flesh. Throughout the Book of Romans, Paul teaches the believers about the war between our flesh (carnal nature) and our spirit man. He so fervently warns us not to allow our 'old nature' of carnality to rule. As believers maturing in the faith of God, it is pivotal to our spiritual growth that we not yield to worldly lusts. The Spirit of Christ dwells in us and empowers us to overcome that unruly and old sinful nature.

At times, I wonder if some so-called Christians are trying to turn the Church into a giant cesspool. Common sense tells us that everyone is not engaging in fornication and idolatry. Personally, I know that I am a blood-washed, spirit-filled, sanctified, water-baptized, son of the living God and I am not the only one.

We certainly should understand that each of us is at a different stage in the process of spiritual growth; therefore we must be careful not to judge others unfairly or have a holier-than-thou attitude. Many church people believe they have reached the epitome of holiness because they are not committing adultery or fornication. These people forget that arrogance, worry, greed, pride, envy, and gossip, which may be prevalent in the carnal believer's mind, are also sins.

When I deliver this type of message from the pulpit, sometimes I look out over the congregation and notice people's faces. People tell on themselves. It's obvious who looks worried and how many people have sweat coming down their faces. I am sure, during these sermons, that some of my members are thinking, *I knew I should have stayed home tonight. I left my dinner to come out and hear this! Bishop was so good last Sunday with his message on "Declaring His Glory." Everyone was shouting, running, and jumping. I thought this was going to be another one of those "running and jumping services," and here he is talking about sin!*

The truth does not always feel good, but as a pastor I must do as Paul did in Acts 20:27 when he said, "For I have not shunned declaring unto you the whole counsel of God." People might not like it, but I must teach not only about the promises of the glory, but also what could hinder the glory from being revealed.

We can not walk in ignorance of what God expects from His people. God says in Hosea 4:6, "My people are destroyed for the lack of knowledge: because thou hast rejected knowledge, I will also reject thee...." So as you can see, according to God's Word, I have a responsibility to teach the whole counsel of God and you have the responsibility to accept the teaching, and live accordingly.

How Could We?

> *What shall we say then?*
> *Shall we continue in sin,*
> *that grace may abound?*
>
> *God forbid. How shall we,*
> *that are dead to sin,*
> *ive any longer therein?*
> *(Romans 6:1–2)*

The apostle Paul essentially is asking, "How could we? How could we ever consider continuing in sin, knowing what our Lord and Savior has done for us?" Once we come into the knowledge of salvation, realizing we are saved by grace through faith in Jesus Christ

(Ephesians 2:8), we are not to continue yielding to sin. As *saved* (that is reborn, regenerated believers) children of God, we are rescued from the bondage and penalty of sin. Because of the Blood of Jesus Christ (finished work of Calvary), we are forgiven of all sin and adopted into the family of God. The gift of salvation is just that—a gift. We did nothing to deserve or earn it; God favored us with His gift of salvation.

Paul admonishes the churches in Rome not to take God's grace for granted. Just because He showed love and kindness towards us (Romans 5:8) does not mean that we should continue those sinful ways. The 'gift' of salvation must be accepted; simply receive what has been offered to you (Acts 16:31, Romans 10:8–10). By accepting and receiving the indwelling of His Spirit, you will be empowered to live a holy life pleasing to God. Psalms 119:9 *TLB* says, "How can a young man stay pure? By reading your word and following its rules."

Believers should strive to become vessels of honor through which the Spirit of the LORD can flow freely. As vessels, we hold His Word in our hearts so that we might not sin against Him (Psalm 119:11). When a child of God is a vessel, the world can look at that individual and see the glory and Word of God come alive in our lives.

Too many Christians are attempting to create "gray" areas, but make no mistake about it—right is still right and wrong is still wrong. There is no such thing as a gray area. Your behavior either lines up with the Word of God or it doesn't. Hebrews 4:12 says:

For the word of God is quick, and powerful, and sharper than any two-edged sword, piercing even to the dividing asunder of soul and spirit, and of the joints and marrow, and is a discerner of the thoughts and intents of the heart.

The Word of God should convict and pierce the conscience of those who are not living in obedience. It is impossible for anyone to be promoted to a higher level of glory when his or her motives are not right in the sight of God.

Anyone who is struggling with issues that get in the way of the glory should be honest about it. James 5:16 encourages us to confess our faults one *to* another and pray one *for* another so that we may be healed (made whole and complete). No one is going to beat up a fellow sister or brother in Christ who has a ways to go. Certainly, we in the body of Christ are supposed to help one another as we move from glory to glory. However, those who pretend to have it all together, when the fact is their house is not in order, are only impeding their own progress. In Galatians 6:1 *TLB*, Paul admonishes the saints to do good and love one another. He says that if a person is overtaken in a fault or sin, those who are godly should gently and humbly restore him, helping him to get back on the right path.

I have areas that I struggle with as any other child of God, but we must all learn how to turn from temptation and do the things that are pleasing to God. Acts 14:15 says:

And saying, Sirs, why do ye these things?
We also are men of like passions with you,
and preach unto you that ye should turn
from these vanities unto the living God,
which made heaven, and earth, and the
sea, and all things that are therein:

No matter how long it takes, our Heavenly Father and Creator will teach us how to overcome any temptation that gets in the way of His glory. When someone is vulnerable in a particular area, the LORD will take that person right back to the place where he or she is struggling, until victory. The LORD knows the person needs to be totally delivered from that particular area of vulnerability before the promotion to the next level of glory.

One day, I had a conversation with a well-known celebrity. He told me, "I don't know why I had to come back to this town. I don't even like this place." I began to pray about this and asked the LORD, "Why did you send him back here?" The LORD answered, "He had to return because this is the place where the devil tried to take his life."

The enemy knew that if this young man lived, he would give the Kingdom of God much glory. He had to get the victory over this spirit of suicide that was trying to destroy him. The LORD said, "Now he is going to give Me the glory right here." This young man returned declaring the glory of God and excelling in his field with a "Thank You Jesus!"

Yes, You Can!

There will be times when you will need to dig deep in your spirit and tell yourself, *Yes, I can!* You must believe that with the help of the LORD you can over-come any temptation of the flesh. Be encouraged by this word from 1 Corinthians 10:13 *TLB* which says, "But remember this—the wrong desires that come into your life aren't anything new or different. Many others have faced exactly the same problems before you. And no temptation is irresistible. You can trust God to keep the temptation from becoming so strong that you can't stand up against it, for he has promised this and will do what he says. He will show you how to escape temptation's power so that you can bear up patiently against it."

Let the world know that you are preparing yourself for greater glory. Be confident because the devil is not big or bad enough to stop what God is getting ready to do through you. It's all for God, but it's happening through us. We are loaded daily with benefits (Psalm 68:19) because He gets glory.

Glory People

Let me describe people who are *destined for glory.* They would rather "fight than switch." They are determined to reach their maximum potential and fulfill their destiny. "Glory people" strive to be the best they can be and never give up. They are not satisfied with just operating a business—they desire a profitable business. They are not content with going through the motions at their job. Glory people aim for the top in their profession. They won't be quiet, sit down, or be satisfied until the glorious power of God is operating mightily in their lives. Glory people will not let the devil put a pacifier in their mouths to shut them up. They are militant and violent if necessary, because they know that "the violent take it by force" (Matthew 11:12b). Do you fit this description?

As a pastor, I am not satisfied with a member's song and hand wave, if that person leaves the sanctuary still physically sick. I will not be satisfied with people who spin around and have perfect church attendance, yet their families are in a mess. I will not be satisfied with anything less than what the Word has declared. If God's Word declared it, then I declare it and won't be content until I see victory manifested in every area.

You might say, "But what about the times when I am experiencing heartaches and pain and it doesn't look like I can make it?" Just remember that God is still God. Tell yourself, "Yes, I can!" Glory people must have tenacity. Know that God has a set time on the clock of Heaven to show forth His glory in your life. Remind yourself, *He is my Helper and I will persevere through these heartaches and pains. Why? Because I am a part of the 'glory people' crowd!*

Fasten Your Seatbelt!

Being changed from glory to glory can be like riding in an aircraft during turbulent weather. When pilots receive information that there is bad weather ahead, they immediately instruct the passengers to return to their seats and fasten their seatbelts. As the aircraft begins to experience turbulence, a call for assistance is made. They request authorization from the air traffic controllers to climb to a higher altitude, high above the storm. Until permission is granted to change altitude, the pilot must hold the aircraft in its present position despite the turbulent weather. Authorization to elevate to a higher altitude is not granted until the way has been cleared. That aircraft must stay in the turbulent weather despite the bumps and jilts. Once authorization has been granted for the aircraft to climb up to a higher altitude, on the way, there may still be some dips and jerks. However, when it finally reaches the desired altitude, the ride is smooth once again.

You might experience rocking and shaking on your way to the next level of glory, but always remember that God will protect you. During those times when you feel like you're coming out of your seat, just fasten your seat belt. This belt is God's Word. Fasten it securely and remain confident that He is in control.

For each level of glory you must endure more turbulence. Sometimes it may appear that you have suffered some losses on this journey, but don't let that disturb you. The worst thing a person can do is stop believing the Word of God as a result of experiencing a difficult situation. All of us go through trials and tribulations, but they are only tests. You cannot get to certain spiritual levels unless you pass each test.

Testing periods equip and prepare us for the next level of glory. The LORD understands that when someone does not successfully pass the test, he or she will probably not be able to stand the blessing. Most people who get blessed without being tested are not able to handle it. They may get lifted up in pride and blow up. But when individuals have been tried, tested, and found true, and know what they had to go through to get where they are, God can take them to greater glory in Him. He knows these believers will not get high-minded and haughty. We realize that it all could be gone in a "New York minute;" therefore we remain humble at His feet. Our focus is on staying in position, and giving God glory.

It's Worth It!

For I reckon that the sufferings of
this present time are not worthy
to be compared with the glory
which shall be revealed in us.
(Romans 8:18)

Believers can be Spirit-filled, speakers with other tongues, shouters, dancers, hand-wavers, aisle-runners, and street witnesses, but I have not found anyone yet, myself included, who likes suffering. Remember, in chapter six of this book, we saw how our Lord and Savior Jesus Christ didn't want to suffer. He even asked God to remove this cup from Him (Luke 22:42). Nobody welcomes suffering; however, in understanding it's purpose, I've learned how to accept it.

Developing an attitude of acceptance is a process that does not come naturally. Some people's first reaction to suffering is not a spiritual one. Often there is no consideration as to whether God is working His glory out through this. We want the trouble to go away and for God to turn it around or cut it off! Or, better yet, simply remove it.

These are the times the enemy tells us, "You better not pray or say anything because you were born a sinner, feel like a sinner, and will always be a sinner. On top of that, you are not filled with the Holy Spirit, and you know you messed up. So shut up." This can be a trying time, but after all the drama has passed, the best thing a believer can do is come back to God. This is when you need to say, "LORD, I want to get to the place in You where I will no longer have a flesh reaction, but a spirit reaction. God, I do not know how You plan to work this out, but I am confident that You will do it. I also know that whatever I must endure is worth it because the suffering of this present time is not worthy to be compared with the glory that shall be revealed in me!" Isaiah 48:10 declares that the children of God are refined in the furnace of affliction. We are purified in the furnace of adversity.

When people tell me about the things they are going through, I listen for their stance. In other words, I want to know how they plan to hold on while they go through the test. My wife puts it eloquently when she asks, "What Scripture are you standing on?" Sometimes the enemy comes against people so strongly that they forget

God's Word. However, one of the worst things people can do is let the enemy's pressure make them forget what God has declared for their lives. The Word of God is our most powerful arsenal in spiritual warfare.

For every trouble we go through, trial we face, and difficulty we must handle, we can say, "It's worth it." We can take it because we have been given the grace to make it through. We can do all things through Christ who strengthens us (Philippians 4:13); therefore we can overcome any obstacle that comes our way. When you stand on His Word and refuse to bow down, the victory will come to your house. Never lower your standards! Be determined and say, "Come what may, I am going to believe God"—you cannot fail. Sometimes we just need to wait, knowing God is faithful to His promises.

God does not always show us the complete map to our destination. If some people knew the details of God's plan and purpose for their lives, they would probably get too excited, and move ahead of His timing. Others would feel so overwhelmed that they may get off the path and therefore delay His timing. Most of the time, we must step out on faith and trust God to lead and direct us. Abraham was called the Father of Faith. Let's look at what Hebrews 11:8 *AMP* says concerning him: "[Urged on] by faith Abraham, when he was called, obeyed and went forth to a place which he was destined to receive as an inheritance; and he went, although he did not know or trouble his mind about where he was to go."

Had Abraham not stepped out on faith, he would not have reached his destiny. If the enemy can make you doubt what God has declared for your life, because of the trouble you face, he'll cause you to live without it. You'll live without the things that have your name on them. You'll die without reflecting the glory God has ordained for you to give Him. By the time my life has ended on this earth, I hope that I have reflected every ounce of glory that God determined I should.

We Rise

Arise, shine; for thy light is come, and the
glory of the LORD is risen upon thee.
(Isaiah 60:1)

The glory of the Lord shall shine magnificently upon those who believe and receive His Word. The children of God, according to Matthew 5:14–16, are the light of the world positioned in high places to shine and radiate brightness to all. As others see our glowing light, they will praise and glorify our Heavenly Father. And we have not seen anything yet because there's more glory on the way. God is going to pour out so much glory on us that the world will come to us and say, "What's that?" Kings, queens, and governors are coming. Congressmen will marvel, "What is it that they have?" We proudly tell them, "It's glory." It's the divine plan, purpose, and will of God being manifested on earth! Come in and let me show you what the LORD has done."

Things will happen for us that cannot be explained because we will live, walk, and move in the favor of God. The LORD will turn things around because He wants us positioned for the glory. You'll meet people and wonder, *How in the world did I meet them?* You will go places and wonder, *How in the world was I able to get here?* For those who are ready, things are going to happen so fast because the glory of God is being magnified and multiplied upon the earth.

Attain the Glory

As we fulfill God's purpose and plan for our lives, we are elevated from *glory to glory* until the same radiant glory that flows from Him shall flow from us. This is the destiny of the believer. This teaching will not affect everyone in a positive way because many people will not receive it in their spirits. From my experience, people look at being transformed into His image in one of two ways. On one hand, many feel it's just too hard to reach, then decide to walk away. On the other hand, we have those who receive the Word and are willing to do what it takes to receive the promises of God.

You might have a ways to go before you attain the glory that God has destined for your life, and there certainly will be obstacles along the way. God is omniscient; therefore, for every trial and tribulation you face, there is a victory already planned (1 Corinthians 10:13). Be encouraged and remember His Word which declares, "He who has begun a good work in you will perform it until the day of Jesus Christ" (Philippians 1:6). For every victory received, there's a level of glory obtained. However, hold on until your change comes! We are being transformed from glory to glory!

In the next chapter, we will take a closer look at the believer's position in the Kingdom of God. We will rejoice in the fact that our Creator could have chosen to express His glory in any number of ways, but He gave this honor to His Son, Jesus Christ; and to everyone who believes in Him. Because of His grace and love for us, believers can fulfill the eternal purpose He declared for us before the foundation of the world. We are destined to be an expression of His glory, in this present age and in the age to come.

EIGHT

CROWNED WITH GLORY AND HONOR

When I consider thy heavens,
the work of thy fingers,
the moon and the stars,
which thou has ordained;

What is man, that thou art mindful
of him? and the son of man,
that thou visitest him?

For thou hast made him a little lower
*than the angels, and hast **crowned him***
with glory and honor.
(Psalm 8:3–5)

Of all God's creations—the heavens, the earth, sun, moon, and stars—He chose to place His crown of glory and honor on man. Mankind was established as the centerpiece and main attraction of all creation. To radiate His glory throughout the universe, we were created, designed, and fashioned in the image and likeness of God.

The psalmist asked, "What is man, that thou art mindful of him? And the son of man, that thou visitest him?" The writer wanted to know why the God of the universe gave man the honor of being the revelation and expression of His glory.

In this chapter, we will examine the psalmist's question. We will study how lucifer, the anointed cherub, lost his place of glory in the heavens and how man was created to fill it as a worshipper of God, the Creator. Because of God's plan to receive glory from our lives, even though satan might try to kill or destroy us, he can't—he is a defeated foe. Our divine destiny shall come to pass. God has crowned us with glory and honor and nothing and no one can take that away.

"I Will Exalt My Throne above the Stars of God"

There are two places in the Bible to which I want to take you. These two places will offer some insight into lucifer's original position in the Kingdom of Heaven and how he lost it. We initially studied this first passage in chapter three. Let's return to Isaiah 14:13–14. It reads:

> *For thou hast said in thine heart, I will
> ascend into heaven, I will exalt my throne*

> *above the stars of God: I will sit also*
> *upon the mount of the congregation,*
> *in the sides of the north:*
>
> *I will ascend above the heights of the*
> *clouds; I will be like the most High.*

The second passage for us to study is found in Ezekiel, chapter 28. Let's begin reading at verse 13:

> *Thou hast been in Eden the garden of*
> *God; every precious stone was thy*
> *covering, the sardius, topaz, and the*
> *diamond, the beryl, the onyx, and the*
> *jasper, the sapphire, the emerald, and the*
> *carbuncle, and gold: the workmanship of*
> *thy tabrets and of thy pipes was prepared*
> *in thee in the day that thou wast created.*

God performed an extraordinary work when He created lucifer. He was adorned with diamonds, sapphires, emeralds, gold, and every other precious stone and his ability to sing was unsurpassed. Lucifer was beautiful to behold and his voice was angelic. Let's continue reading Ezekiel 28.

Verse 14–15:

> *Thou art the anointed cherub*
> *that covereth; and I have set thee so:*
> *thou wast upon the holy mountain of God;*
> *thou hast walked up and down*
> *in the midst of the stones of fire.*

*Thou wast perfect in thy ways from the
day that thou wast created, till iniquity
was found in thee.*

As the "anointed cherub that covereth," lucifer held one of the highest positions in the heavens. His position allowed him to be in God's presence and to observe His ways. This anointed angel originally operated in his purpose, in a perfect manner. Please be reminded that anything God created is good, and this angel was no exception. He was a created being—an angel. Perfect in his ways, he was whole and undefiled without a blemish or spot until iniquity was found in him. Let's continue reading.

Verse 16–17:

*By the multitude of thy merchandise
they have filled the midst of thee
with violence, and thou hast sinned:
therefore I will cast thee as profane
out of the mountain of God:
and I will destroy thee,
O covering cherub,
from the midst of the stones of fire.*

*Thine heart was lifted up
because of thy beauty, thou hast
corrupted thy wisdom by reason of
thy brightness: I will cast thee
to the ground, I will lay thee before kings,
that they may behold thee.*

The beauty, riches, and glory God had given lucifer were more than he could handle. Instead of using them to glorify God, he became self-exalted. Pride will proceed destruction, as our Creator will not allow us to think we are self-sufficient. Lucifer proclaimed, "I will exalt my throne above the stars of God." God stripped him of everything he once possessed and cast him out of Heaven.

The LORD made man and gave him every honor and glory that once belonged to the former covering cherub, now the fallen angel. God said:

> *Let us make man in our image,*
> *after our likeness: and let them*
> *have dominion over the fish of the sea,*
> *and over the fowl of the air,*
> *and over the cattle, and over all the earth,*
> *and over every creeping thing*
> *that creepeth upon the earth.*
> *(Genesis 1:26)*

God made, blessed, and empowered man, giving him dominion over everything upon the earth. Man had everything he would ever need or desire—even things he couldn't imagine. Then the LORD gave man one of the greatest gifts of all; He *crowned him with glory and honor.*

When the enemy sees us reflecting the glory of God, he is reminded that we now possess a position he once held. Never again can lucifer reflect God's glory! He knows that the radiant brightness he wore at one time is forever gone. He is darkness, never to shine again.

We are living in a time of an increasing intensity of God's glory being revealed through the body of Christ. Satan knows his time is growing short and that the season for believers to move into our "pre-determined moment" has come. However, before I go any further, let me issue a warning: moving closer to our destiny does not mean things are going to get easier. As a matter of fact, this is usually the time when all hell breaks loose! The enemy gets mad and causes more turmoil when he sees believers getting close to the place where we will put on the glory and splendor he once possessed.

Eden

Ezekiel 28:13 tells us that lucifer was in Eden, the garden of God. Man was placed in Eden by God and the enemy showed up to do whatever he could to take away the glory. Please take note that the devil makes a point of showing up any place where the glory of God is operating.

Eden is derived from the Hebrew word for "delight" or "pleasure." Thus, Eden is often thought of as a wealthy, luxurious paradise full of pleasure for its inhabitants. Historians, geographers, and theologians have not been able to locate a definite physical place called Eden. However, the Bible does provide some clues as to where Eden may possibly be located.

Genesis 2:10–14 tells us that there was one major river that flowed from Eden to water the garden. Four rivers flowed out of this major river: the Pishon, the Gihon, the Hiddekel (Tigris), and the Euphrates. We know that the Tigris and Euphrates are the two great rivers of ancient Mesopotamia (present-day Iraq), so many have concluded that Eden was located in this general area. The important issue here is that Eden was a place of God's continual presence. God strategically placed Adam and Eve in an environment where they could continually abide in His glorious presence.

The serpent deceived Eve in the Garden of Eden. The Bible describes the serpent as being more *subtle*, meaning "shrewd" or "crafty" than any beast of the field which the LORD God had made (Genesis 3:1). To get Eve's attention, the serpent probably presented himself as being on the same level as God. Satan continues to operate in the same spirit of pride and self-exaltation exhibited in Heaven before he was kicked out. Surely, he made it seem as if he knew everything about God. Satan is a master of deception and will talk as if he were God. This is why it is so important to "believe not every spirit, but try the spirits whether they are of God" (1 John 4:1).

When people say, "God told me this" or "God told me that," I am often apprehensive because some people do not know whether they heard from the Spirit of God or from the devil. The serpent will tell people whatever they want to hear to draw them away from God's purpose and plan.

Eve was seduced by her own lust. The serpent told Eve, in Genesis 3:5, that God forbade her from eating the fruit because, "In the day ye eat thereof, then your eyes shall be opened, and ye shall be as gods, knowing good and evil." Knowing good and evil and being exalted as gods sounded good to Eve. The trap was laid and she fell into it. Eve's focus shifted from obeying and glorifying God to satisfying herself; she was enticed by the thought of being as a god. She thought, *You mean, I will be wise and knowledgeable?* Eve's lust and Adam's willingness to follow after what she did caused them to depart from the plan of God.

The things the enemy says usually have some element of twisted truth to them. That's why he's called a deceiver and a liar (Revelation 12:9, John 8:44). He may speak part of the truth, but it is neither the whole truth nor the plan of God. What the serpent told Eve would happen, if she ate the forbidden fruit, was partially correct. God Himself said, "Behold, the man is become as one of us" (Genesis 3:22). Unfortunately, the serpent left out the rest of the story. The devil didn't tell the man and his wife the part about losing their honor and glory and being driven out of the Garden.

The Last Adam

The same spirit of deception that was used to take the glory from the first Adam was tried on the last Adam—our Lord and Savior Jesus Christ. Let's go to Matthew, chapter 4.

Verses 1–3:

> *Then was Jesus led up of the Spirit into the wilderness to be tempted of the devil.*

> *And when he had fasted*
> *forty days and forty nights,*
> *he was afterward an hungered.*

> *And when the tempter came to him,*
> *he said, **If thou be** the Son of God,*
> *command that these stones*
> *be made bread.*

When the tempter approached Jesus, he said, "If thou be," meaning, if you are. If you recall, he told Eve, "You shall be;" that is, you will become. The devil knew who Jesus was so he did not say, "Shall;" he said, "If." Satan tried to intimidate Jesus by getting Him to prove that He was the Son of God. The devil taunted, "If you really are the Son of God, surely you can command that these stones be made into bread." Jesus did not fall for the adversary's trick. In verse 4, Jesus responded using the Word of God:

> *It is written, Man shall not live by bread*
> *alone, but by every word that*
> *proceedeth out of the mouth of God.*

The devil did not give up and the next passage shows us just how shrewd he can be. This time he uses Scripture to back up his deception.

Verses 5–11:

> *Then the devil taketh him up*
> *into the holy city, and setteth him*
> *on a pinnacle of the temple,*

*And saith unto him, **If thou be***
the Son of God, cast thyself down:
***for it is written**, He shall give*
his angels charge concerning thee:
and in their hands they shall
bear thee up, lest at any time
thou dash thy foot against a stone.

Jesus said unto him,
It is written again,
Thou shalt not tempt
the Lord thy God.

Again, the devil taketh him up
into an exceeding high mountain,
and showeth him all the kingdoms
of the world, and the glory of them;

And saith unto him,
All these things
will I give thee, if thou wilt
fall down and worship me.

Then saith Jesus unto him,
Get thee hence, Satan:
for it is written,
Thou shalt worship
the Lord thy God, and him only
shalt thou serve.

Then the devil leaveth him,
and, behold, angels came
and ministered unto him.

The devil was essentially preaching when he said, "For it is written." He continued his efforts to tempt Jesus with pretty pictures and half-truths. The devil showed Jesus the kingdoms of this world and told Him, in essence, "Don't you want this? I will give it all to you if you fall down and worship me." Again, we see a demonstration of the same spirit of self-exaltation that was at work in Ezekiel 28:12–18 and Genesis 3:1–5. However, our Lord and Savior knew and embraced the *true* Word of God and the devil had to flee.

The enemy makes a big mistake anytime he tries to stop God's glory from coming forth through those ordained before the foundation of the world. Whatever the enemy uses for our destruction, God turns it around and uses it to fulfill His purpose and plan. The adversary made a fatal error when he crucified our Lord and Savior. The devil thought he had succeeded in tearing down the Kingdom of God and putting out the light of His glory. However, quite the opposite was true. Jesus said:

> *And I, if and when I am*
> *lifted up from the earth*
> *[on the cross], will draw*
> *and attract all men*
> *[Gentiles as well as Jews] to Myself.*
> *(John 12:32, The Amplified Bible)*

Our Lord and Savior was saying, in effect, "Do with Me what you want, but when I am risen, I shall have all power and great glory." Matthew 24:30 and 28:18 tells us:

And then shall appear the sign
of the Son of man in heaven:
and then shall all the tribes
of the earth mourn, and they
shall see the Son of man coming
in the clouds of heaven
with power and great glory.

And Jesus came and spake unto them,
saying, All power is given unto me
in heaven and in earth.

The enemies of Christ did not understand that when they crucified Jesus, His glory and honor would be multiplied; what they meant for bad, God meant for good. He became the firstborn of many brethren who would also be *destined for glory* (Romans 8:29). When the princes of this world hung our Lord on the cross, the way was paved for many to be redeemed, regenerated, and transformed believers ready for His glory (Hebrews 2:9–10).

Our Hope Is in The Lord

The hope or expected end of the believer must be based on the promise of God's Word. Many times we become disillusioned because people, who we thought would always be there for us, reject us, persecute us or even try to kill us. We should not lose faith when it is our best friend or even a relative who comes against us. Just remember: the enemy may try to strip you of your glory by snatching away your family, finances, friends, or faith. But he can't! Despite any humiliation or embarrassment you've endured, the glory of God will be with you no matter where you land.

Mature believers are able to praise the Lord at all times because we understand that the devil cannot take the glory. The adversary is looking at many of us and saying, "Don't they realize they are in a pit? Doesn't she realize I have her in bondage? Doesn't he realize I have him in slavery?" Even if the enemy has us in a place where we do not belong, the glory will still be upon us. Let satan know that no matter what he takes from us or how he tries to scandalize us, he cannot keep us from our glorious destiny. Our hope and confidence has always been in the Lord for He *is* our glory and the lifter up of our heads (Psalm 3:3).

God knew about the trouble that each of us would face before we were conceived in our mother's womb. Believers who realize that our trials, and tribulations— as well as our breakthroughs, and miracles were spoken forth and declared before the foundation of the world—will have a power and connection with God that the enemy cannot handle.

There will be people who see you moving in the glory of God and not like it. They do not understand that you are only coming into your predetermined moment. They may see the blessings coming your way and try to stop them. They think, *Let's see how strong he is when I walk out on him. Let's see how blessed she feels when I tell her friends her business.* My advice is to just keep moving in His glory because there is not a thing anyone can do about it. Declare Genesis 50:20, "But as for you, ye thought evil against me: but God meant it unto good..."

As we continue to walk in our destiny, the glory of God will grow stronger in our lives. As David said in Psalm 8:4–6 *AMP*, "What is man that You are mindful of him, and the son of [earthborn] man that You care for him? Yet You have made him but a little lower than God [or heavenly beings], and You have **crowned him with glory and honor**. You made him to have **dominion** over the works of your hands; You have put all things under his feet:"

He has *crowned us with glory and honor* so that He is glorified. What a privilege it is for us to have power, dominion, and authority over the awesome work of God's hand. All things are under our feet. Just as Scripture tells us in 1 Corinthians 2:8—had the rulers and accusers of our Lord and Savior Jesus Christ known the 'outcome' of His death, they never would have crucified Him. The writer of the Book of Hebrews 2:9 stated that before the Calvary Cross experience Jesus was ranked man, a little lower than angels, but afterwards was crowned with glory and honour. After suffering as the Sacrificial Lamb of God, all power was given unto Him!" Because of the death of Jesus Christ, all men can freely fellowship with God, resulting in a growing body of glorified believers who bring forth His will on earth. God's purpose and plan for man shall be fulfilled, in this present age and through eternity. *To God be the glory!*

In chapter nine, we will explore the manifested presence of God and how it relates to reaching our destiny. Most people who successfully fulfill God's purpose for their lives understand that without His presence, they would surely fail. I plan to demonstrate how His presence is necessary to strengthen and guide us to our divine destination. We need His presence to bless and keep us on this journey. Come with me, and enter into the presence of the LORD.

NINE

HIS PRESENCE

Declare his glory among the heathen;
his marvellous works
among all nations.

For great is the LORD,
and greatly to be praised:
he also is to be feared above all gods.

For all the gods of the people
are idols: but the LORD
made the heavens.

Glory and honour are in his presence;
strength and gladness are in his place.
Give unto the LORD,
ye kindreds of the people,
give unto the LORD
glory and strength.

Give unto the LORD the glory due
unto his name: bring an offering,
and come before him:
worship the LORD
in the beauty of holiness.
(1 Chronicles 16:24–29)

It is only through the presence of the LORD that we will be able to successfully fulfill God's purpose and plan for our lives. In His presence we are equipped, sustained, and blessed with everything needed to defeat the enemy and reach our divine destiny. Glory and honor are ours, in His presence. We find strength and gladness in His sanctuary. Souls are saved, bodies are healed, and the captives are set free in the presence of the LORD.

Glory is the manifested presence of the divine attributes and perfections of God. Unfortunately, many in the body of Christ lack understanding about His presence and, consequently, are hesitant to pursue it. They do not realize that if they acknowledge Him as *Jehovah-Shalom*, the LORD God our Peace, His presence will give them peace which passeth all understanding (Philippians 4:7). They do not tap into the power that comes from entering the presence of *Jehovah-Rapha*, our Healer and *Jehovah-Jireh,* our Provider. They miss out on experiencing *Jehovah-Shammah*—the LORD who IS omnipresent and will never leave nor forsake us. In this chapter, we will study His presence, a dimension of God's glory that believers can enter and receive everything we need to reach our destiny.

The Glory Cloud

Scripture often talks about the glory of the LORD appearing as a cloud. The presence of the cloud was indicative of God's presence. It's helpful to understand the glory and presence of God using clouds as an analogy. Most of us have heard of cumulus, cirrus, and stratus clouds. As these clouds move across bodies of water, they take up moisture. They actually absorb water from the oceans, seas, and rivers. When a cloud is filled, it releases the accumulated moisture in the form of rain.

Think of the presence of God as a 'glory cloud'. When the glory cloud moves among the people, we should send up praises and glorify Him. Just as the moisture that rises and fills the clouds is released back to the earth, when the LORD is filled with our praises and glory, He will shower us with His glory.

I believe as I send up praises, God rains down blessings. Furthermore, it is important to realize that when the blessings do come, they are not going to fall only on me. The blessings will fall on everyone in His presence. Lot, Abraham's nephew, is a good example. We all know that Abraham was the one who God chose to bless. However, since Lot was close to Abraham, when Heaven rained on Abraham, Lot was rained on too!

King David said it this way: "O magnify the LORD with me, and let us exalt His name together" (Psalm 34:3). Believers who want God's glory and honor poured on them must send glory and honor up to Him. This is not the time to be cool, calm, and collected. We need too much from God to be reserved and cute. It's time to magnify the LORD and declare His glory in the earth.

Let's take a moment to study a few of the ancient prophets' accounts of being in the presence of the LORD. In the Book of Isaiah, chapter 6, Isaiah said:

> *In the year that King Uzziah died*
> *I saw also the Lord sitting upon a throne,*
> *high and lifted up, and his train*
> *filled the temple.*
>
> *Above it stood the seraphims: each one*
> *had six wings; with twain he covered his*
> *face, and with twain he covered his feet,*
> *and with twain he did fly.*
>
> *And one cried unto another, and said,*
> *Holy, holy, holy, is the LORD of hosts:*
> *the whole earth is full of his glory.*
> *(vv. 1–3)*

In this vision, Isaiah saw the *Shekinah* (the glory/divine presence of God) fill the heavenly temple. In His presence the angels cried out to one another and said, "Holy, holy, holy is the LORD of hosts: the whole earth is full of his glory." Another illustration of the effect of being in God's presence is found in 1 Kings 8:10–11. It reads:

> *And it came to pass, when the priests were*
> *come out of the holy place, that the cloud*
> *filled the house of the LORD,*

So that the priests could not stand to
minister because of the cloud:
for the glory of the LORD had filled
the house of the LORD.

In this Scripture passage, King Solomon and the entire congregation of Israel were gathered together to dedicate the newly constructed temple. The priests had just placed the Ark of the Covenant in the holy of holies, when the glory of the LORD filled the temple. The presence of the LORD was so powerful that the priests could not stand to minister. 2 Chronicles 5:13–14 provides additional information about what happened during the service. It reads:

It came even to pass, as the trumpeters
and singers were as one, to make one
sound to be heard in praising and
thanking the LORD; and when they lifted
up their voice with the trumpets and
cymbals and instruments of music,
and praised the LORD, saying, For he is
good; for his mercy endureth for ever:
that then the house was filled with a
cloud, even the house of the LORD;

So that the priests could not stand
to minister by reason of the cloud:
for the glory of the LORD had
filled the house of God.

Here, we learn that the singers and musicians were with one accord, praising and thanking the LORD when everything came to a stop. The glory of God was so intense that the priests could not continue with their program. All they could do was bow down under the cloud of His presence. It is in this place of the powerful presence of God when miracles and wonders happen.

In 2 Chronicles 7:1–3, God made His presence known in a mighty way. This passage reads:

Now when Solomon had made an end
of praying, the fire came down from
heaven, and consumed the burnt offering
and the sacrifices; and the glory
of the LORD filled the house.

And the priests could not enter into the
house of the LORD, because the glory of
the LORD had filled the LORD'S house.

And when all the children of Israel saw
how the fire came down, and the glory
of the LORD upon the house,
they bowed themselves with their faces
to the ground upon the pavement,
and worshipped, and praised the LORD,
saying, For he is good;
for his mercy endureth for ever.

Fire from Heaven came down and consumed the burnt offering and sacrifices that were on the altar. Once again the glory of the LORD filled the house and the priests were unable to enter. When the people saw the glory of the LORD upon the temple, all they could do was lie prostrate on the ground and continue worshipping and praising Him.

A Spiritual Place

We must comprehend that we need His presence to obtain our destiny. The presence of God is a spiritual place where His thoughts, plan, and purpose are illuminated in our spirit. Here, the atmosphere is most ripe for lives to be transformed. Divine help is summoned as God commands His angelic host on our behalf, so that no obstacle can hinder us from fulfilling our purpose.

Many believers can personally relate to the awesome and profound effect being in His presence has upon us. When the glory of the LORD is in the sanctuary, it is almost impossible to just sit and gaze and be ambivalent about what is happening. When people enter into His presence, their legs might get weak. Hands often go up in the air and tears roll down their eyes. Heads may be lifted up toward Heaven or humbly bowed down. Some people may kneel before the LORD while others choose to lay prostrate. We may hear words of thanksgiving, honor, adoration, and even repentance being uttered. And others may be in total awe and unable to speak any words, but yet have an attitude of worship. Even those who may not have confessed Jesus Christ as Lord and Savior will usually "feel something."

During these intimate moments, people might look at you as if something is wrong. If you get the opportunity, just let these individuals know that contrary to what they were thinking, you were not in any pain and nothing was wrong. They should know that what they observed was the overwhelming and overpowering desire to worship that comes from being in His presence.

Expect God to Show Up

Sometimes I wonder if the saints of God are really coming to church expecting Him to show up. Many church people seem to be looking at what others are doing or saying rather than moving in and experiencing the flow of His glory. I find that those who reverence His presence pay no attention to what's happening around them. People truly experiencing His presence are not focusing on how they look, where they are, or what the time is. When believers reach this level of intimacy with the LORD, their focus is on glorifying Him.

Moses' Request

Moses personally experienced the power of the presence of the LORD on numerous occasions. He was an eyewitness to the plagues that came upon the Egyptians and the subsequent release of the children of Israel. He saw the LORD part the Red Sea with a strong east wind, so the children of Israel could escape the Egyptians by crossing on dry land. When the LORD called him up to the top of Mount Sinai to commune with Him and be in His presence, Moses came down from the mountain with the Ten Commandments.

In Exodus, chapter 33, we find Moses at a critical stage in his life where he is being used intensely by God. He was in the middle of leading the children of Israel into the Promised Land when he made a request of God. The people had just sinned by worshipping the golden calf and Moses interceded for them. Because of his intercession, God spared their lives. Their conversation:

Now therefore, I pray thee,
if I have found grace in thy sight,
shew me now thy way, that I may know
thee, that I may find grace in thy sight:
and consider that this nation is thy people.

And he said, My presence shall
go with thee, and I will give thee rest.

And he said unto him, If thy presence
go not with me, carry us not up hence.

For wherein shall it be known here
that I and thy people have found grace
in thy sight? Is it not in that thou
goest with us? So shall we be separated,
I and thy people, from all the people
that are upon the face of the earth.

And the LORD said unto Moses,
I will do this thing also that thou
hast spoken: for thou hast found
grace in my sight,
and I know thee by name.
(Exodus 33:13–17)

147

Moses knew he could not lead this stubborn people without God's presence. Moses wanted assurance that the children of Israel had the favor and grace needed to enter the Promised Land and fulfill their destiny. Moses said, in essence, "Look God, if the world is going to see that You are with us, then show us Your favor in such a magnificent way that the difference between Your people and the world will be so obvious that anybody can see it. We need to see an absolute burst of Your power. We want to see an absolute explosion of Your majesty. There's no other way that the people already living in the land will know that we are Your people unless they see Your presence with us." Verse 17 lets us know that God granted Moses' request.

You can ask God for His presence to be with us just as Moses did. This glorious connection with God sets us apart from the rest of the world. Don't hesitate to tell the LORD: "I want You to move in my life so powerfully that when the people of the world see me, they will say that I am more than just a lucky man/woman who has himself/herself together." People will notice—there is something about that person. Everything that the hands touch gets blessed. It does not make any difference what comes, this person still comes out on top in everything!

Show Me Your Glory

Next, Moses asked, "I beseech thee, shew me thy glory" (Exodus 33:18). Moses had seen God do many miraculous things, but he wanted to personally see God expressed and manifested in all His glory. The LORD responded by saying:

> *I will make all my goodness pass before*
> *thee, and I will proclaim the name of the*
> *LORD before thee; and will be gracious to*
> *whom I will be gracious, and will*
> *shew mercy on whom I will shew mercy.*
>
> *And he said, Thou canst not see my face:*
> *for there shall no man see me, and live.*
>
> *And the LORD said, Behold,*
> *there is a place by me, and*
> *thou shalt stand upon a rock:*
>
> *And it shall come to pass, while my glory*
> *passeth by, that I will put thee in a clift*
> *of the rock, and will cover thee*
> *with my hand while I pass by:*
>
> *And I will take away mine hand,*
> *and thou shalt see my back parts:*
> *but my face shall not be seen.*
> *(Exodus 33:19–23)*

It is always a privilege and an honor when the LORD allows us to experience His presence. No man can physically see His face and live, but we can spiritually see and feel His glory. His presence changes the atmosphere. His glory changes situations. The glory of God causes the immutable Word of God to be manifested in our lives.

Abide in His Presence

Abiding in the presence of the LORD is pivotal as we seek to know His will for our lives. It is in His presence that we are able to successfully fulfill divine purpose. His presence gives us direction so that we operate in a godly manner at all times. As we do this, glory and honor will be ours. We will experience His abundance, majesty, magnificence, and radiant brilliance.

I want to return one last time to the Garden of Eden. No child of God should ever think he or she has to leave God's presence and go to the enemy for the things they need or desire. When our heart's desires line up with God's desires, He will give them to us because He gets the glory.

The serpent was able to convince Eve that he was willing to offer her something that God would not. Eve was tricked into eating the forbidden fruit because she thought it offered her something that God did not want her to have. In her lustful desire to be as wise as God, Eve forgot about the *Tree of Life* that had everything she could ever imagine or desire.

When Eve ate the fruit of the *Tree of the Knowledge of Good and Evil*, the implications of her decision involved much more than eating a physical piece of fruit. Eve was making a spiritual decision. That spiritual decision was to follow God or the devil. Eve chose sin and death to get what only life could give. If she had chosen the Tree of Life, Adam and Eve would have fulfilled their destiny and had everything they desired.

Take, Eat

John 1:4 says, "In him was life; and the life was the light of men." Acts 5:27-30 reads:

> *And when they had brought them,*
> *they set them before the council:*
> *and the high priest asked them,*

> *Saying, Did not we straitly command you*
> *that ye should not teach in this name?*
> *and, behold, ye have filled Jerusalem*
> *with your doctrine, and intend*
> *to bring this man's blood upon us.*

> *Then Peter and the other apostles*
> *answered and said, We ought to*
> *obey God rather than men.*

> *The God of our fathers raised up Jesus,*
> *whom ye slew and hanged on a tree.*

It is not a coincidence that Jesus is the "life" that was put on the tree and that man must come through Him to be acceptable to God and enter His presence. Even though the adversary was successful in temporarily disturbing the plan, purpose, and will of God for mankind, the LORD provided another life that would be hung on a tree to redeem us.

> *And as they were eating, Jesus took bread,*
> *and blessed it, and brake it,*
> *and gave it to the disciples, and said,*
> ***Take, eat**; this is my body.*
> *(Matthew 26:26)*

Believers can eat freely from the Tree of Life that has every good gift and blessing. We do not have to pursue the devil to get something God said we could have—all we have to do is choose life! "Seek ye first the kingdom of God, and his righteousness; and all these things shall be added unto you" (Matthew 6:33).

You Are the Temple of God

Know ye not that ye are the temple of God,
and that the Spirit of God dwelleth in you?
(1 Corinthians 3:16)

Ezekiel had a vision of the glory of God as represented by a strong wind, cloud, and fire (Ezekiel, chapter 1). He also saw God's glory leaving Israel at the destruction of the first Temple (Ezekiel 10:18–19). Many are still praying for the return of the *Shekinah*. However, believers know about the day when a group of followers of Jesus Christ were with one accord in one place and "suddenly there came a sound from Heaven as of a rushing mighty wind, and it filled the whole house where they were sitting" (Acts 2:1–2). The *Shekinah* returned on the day of Pentecost and not only filled the place, it filled the people and they began to speak with other tongues, as the Spirit gave them utterance (Acts 2:3).

Psalm 16:11 reads:

Thou wilt shew me the path of life: in thy
presence is fulness of joy; at thy right
hand there are pleasures for evermore.

The temple in Jerusalem has long been destroyed. In this divine time on the clock of Heaven, believers are temples of God, and His spirit dwells in us. When we allow His presence to dwell in us and begin to operate our day to day lives according to His will, His ways, His purpose and His plan, the path of life that God has prepared for us will be made known. In the presence of the LORD, we will receive spiritual illumination and revelation knowledge shall be made clear. It's all part of fulfilling His purpose and plan for our lives.

In the next chapter, I will discuss the manifested power of God in the life of the believer. God is omnipresent. He is also omnipotent; and He can therefore manifest His power in tangible, visible form when He so chooses. What a mighty God we serve! If God is for us, who can be against us?

TEN

THE MANIFESTED POWER OF GOD

He that committeth sin is of the devil;
for the devil sinneth from the beginning.
For this purpose the Son of God
was manifested, that he might destroy
the works of the devil.
(1 John 3:8)

The word *manifest* means to make clear or evident, to show or to reveal. When something has been manifested, it is readily perceived by the senses, especially the sight sense. What was once hidden is now revealed and made clear.

The above Scripture tells of our Lord's manifestation from the spirit to the natural realm. Jesus came from Heaven to earth to reverse and utterly destroy every act the devil perpetrated against mankind. The Son of God became flesh and dwelt among men demonstrating

God's power and authority over all things. Then Jesus made the ultimate sacrifice that resulted in the complete victory over the devil. Hebrews 2:14 says:

> *Forasmuch then as the children are*
> *partakers of flesh and blood, he also himself*
> *likewise took part of the same; that*
> *through death he might destroy him that*
> *had the power of death, that is, the devil;*

The same power that was given to our Lord and Savior has been given to us, so that we may become the sons of God (John 1:12) and fulfill our purpose. Paul describes the magnitude of this power in his letter to the church at Ephesus:

> *And what is the exceeding greatness of his*
> *power to us-ward who believe, according to*
> *the working of his mighty power,*
>
> *Which he wrought in Christ, when he raised*
> *him from the dead, and set him at his own*
> *right hand in the heavenly places,*
>
> *Far above all principality, and power,*
> *and might, and dominion, and every name*
> *that is named, not only in this world, but*
> *also in that which is to come:*
>
> *And hath put all things under his feet,*
> *and gave him to be the head over*
> *all things to the church,*
>
> *Which is his body, the fulness of him that*
> *filleth all in all.*
> *(Ephesians 1:19–23)*

The incomparable power of God that raised Jesus from the dead has been given to the body of Christ to do the will of the Father. Every principality, power, might, dominion, and name has been put under our Lord's feet and ours (Psalm 8:6). It's a spiritual exchange of authority from Heaven to the Church that exists now and forever more.

In this chapter we will explore the revealed, clearly visible, and readily perceived (manifested) power of God that brings forth His will on earth, as it is in Heaven. We will discuss incidences that leave no doubt that "God did it." The body of Christ must never underestimate the LORD's willingness to move powerfully on our behalf. God will do whatever it takes to make sure we obtain our destiny. No weapon that is formed against us can prosper. We will also see how our Lord and Savior came to destroy every work the devil concocted to compromise God's purpose and plan for our lives. And in case the enemy forgets, the One who controls the universe will quickly remind him that he can only go so far. Our God is the final authority on all matters concerning His people. To Him be all blessing, glory, honor, and power forever!

The Name of Jesus

There is no question that God has provided us with the power and authority we need to fulfill our destiny (Ephesians 1:19), but we must know how to access it. This power and authority is available to us through

His Son, Jesus Christ. Let's study this further. Matthew 28:18 reads:

> *And Jesus came and spake unto them,*
> *saying, All power [authority] is given*
> *unto me in heaven and in earth.*

Jesus made the above statement after His resurrection. He told His disciples, in essence, "The Father has given Me all authority both in heaven and in earth." Let's read Philippians 2:9–12:

> *Wherefore God also hath highly exalted him,*
> *and given him a name*
> *which is above every name:*
>
> *That at **the name of Jesus** every knee*
> *should bow, of things in heaven, and things*
> *in earth, and things under the earth;*
>
> *And that every tongue should confess*
> *that Jesus Christ is Lord,*
> *to the glory of God the Father.*

The Name of Jesus was given to the body of Christ to provide direct access to our Heavenly Father. It releases His power and authority. Jesus' Name brings forth the manifested power of God, revealing His might and strength. Calling on the Name, which is above every name, paves the way for God's will to dominate and control any situation.

Trust Him

It does not pay to give lip service concerning the things God has declared for your life. If you are trusting God, don't just say it, really trust Him. Let nothing diminish the power of God in your mind. Regardless of what you are going through, He can bring you to victory.

For every life situation there is someone who can say, "Let me show you the evidence of what God did for me." When you need the LORD to manifest His power on your behalf; find someone who has been through what you are experiencing and who has the testimony, "God did that for me." If you need healing, find someone whom God has healed. If your family needs a money miracle, reach out to the family whose finances have been blessed.

We serve a God who will do it! Though He is Spirit, He will give us an answer that our physical senses can perceive. Yet, let me insert a word of caution at this point: being aware of God's manifested power does not mean that believers can just sit back and not be vigilant concerning the enemy. We must never forget that the adversary is also a spirit whose actions can have a detrimental effect on our lives. The devil causes confusion, grief, and pain, which are evident in the physical realm. In circumstances like these, we must remember God's Word in 1 John 3:8, which says:

> *...For this purpose the Son of God*
> *was manifested, that He might*
> *destroy the works of the devil.*

Whatever the devil has done that manifested negatively in your life, our spiritual God will manifest a physical blessing that will knock the devil out! The Name of

Jesus is powerful enough to pull down any stronghold, and stop any spirit that tries to come against us.

Mature believers who know how to access God's power do not resort to kicking and screaming when trouble comes. We have learned that worrying and throwing tantrums get us nowhere. Believers who may not have attained this level of maturity sometimes try to appear as if they have faith in the power of God. These people have gone to church and studied the look of seasoned believers to the point where they know how to "look" the part. But there will come a time when they find out that the look is not enough—they need the power and authority of the Name of Jesus. They need to know how to call on the Name that causes God's spiritual power to transcend into physical evidence and take care of any problem at hand.

Not everyone can use the Name of Jesus and get results. One must be in position and in right relationship with Him to access His power. This is why it is important to ask the LORD to search us from the crown of our heads to the soles of our feet. We need Him to break down everything that is not like Him so that nothing hinders our access to Him. Sometimes we need to look at ourselves and request that the light from Heaven shine on us. Many of us will reach the same conclusion Isaiah did when he said, "Woe is me! for I am undone; because I am a man of unclean lips, and I dwell in the midst of a people of unclean lips: for mine eyes have seen the King, the LORD of hosts" (Isaiah 6:5).

Be Careful

> *Therefore, my dear ones, as you have*
> *always obeyed [my suggestions], so now, not*
> *only [with the enthusiasm you would show]*
> *in my presence but much more because I am*
> *absent, work out (cultivate, carry out to the*
> *goal, and fully complete) your own salvation*
> *with reverence and awe and trembling*
> *(self-distrust, with serious caution,*
> *tenderness of conscience, watchfulness*
> *against temptation, timidly shrinking from*
> *whatever might offend God and*
> *discredit the name of Christ).*
>
> *[Not in your own strength] for it is God Who*
> *is all the while effectually at work in you*
> *[energizing and creating in you the power*
> *and desire], both to will and to work for*
>
> *His good pleasure and*
> *satisfaction and delight.*
> *(Philippians 2:12–13, The Amplified Bible)*

Pursuing destiny is a very serious matter; far too much is at stake for anyone to be inattentive or lackadaisical about it. Paul warned the Philippians to be careful and never offend God or discredit the Name of Christ in any manner. As we work out our own salvation (destiny) with diligence and an unrelenting attitude, the LORD Himself empowers and motivates us. We will see His manifested power because it is His good pleasure that every promise He declared for us be manifested.

Unfortunately, the enemy has deceived many people into believing that they can obtain blessings without pursuing the "Blessor." To a certain degree, there is some truth in that statement because all of us were blessed before we ever pursued God. However, once we came to know Him as our personal Lord and Savior, we discovered that there were no limits to how far we could go in Him. We realized that He has many blessings for us, but we must properly position ourselves to obtain them. Personally, I want the blessing of being saved. I want the blessing of knowing Jesus in the pardoning of my sin. I want *The Blessing of Commitment* that releases wealth and riches into my life.

God's Power in Action

I want to take you to two passages in the Book of Acts. No message is complete if one cannot provide biblical examples proving that the principles presented are true. These passages illustrate the manifested power of God operating in the lives of those who have aligned themselves with His purpose and plan. Acts 3:1–7 reads:

Now Peter and John went up together
into the temple at the hour of prayer,
being the ninth hour. And a certain man
lame from his mother's womb was carried,
whom they laid daily at the gate of the
temple which is called Beautiful,
to ask alms of them that entered into the
temple; Who seeing Peter and John about
to go into the temple asked an alms.

And Peter, fastening his eyes
upon him with John, said,
Look on us. And he gave heed unto them,
expecting to receive something of them.

Then Peter said, Silver and gold
have I none; but such as I have
give I thee: In the name of Jesus Christ
of Nazareth **rise up and walk.**

And he took him by the right hand,
and lifted him up:
and immediately his feet and
ankle bones received strength.

Now let's read Acts 4:7–10:

And when they had set them in the midst,
they asked, By what power,
or by what name, have ye done this?

Then Peter, filled with the Holy Ghost,
said unto them, Ye rulers of the people,
and elders of Israel, If we this day
be examined of the good deed done
to the impotent man, by what means
he is made whole;

Be it known unto you all, and to all the
people of Israel, that **by the**
name of Jesus Christ of Nazareth,
whom ye crucified, whom God raised from
the dead, even by him doth this man
stand here before you whole.

163

These passages show God's manifested power in action. A man who had been lame from birth was healed by the power of God through Peter. The rulers and elders of the people of Israel who witnessed this miracle asked Peter by what power or name was this man made whole? Peter responded, "By the Name of Jesus Christ of Nazareth." It is God's will, purpose, and plan that the Church be able to say, "By the Name of Jesus Christ." Let's continue reading.

> *And beholding the man which was healed*
> *standing with them,* ***they could say***
> ***nothing against it.***
>
> *But when they had commanded them to*
> *go aside out of the council,*
> *they conferred among themselves,*
>
> *Saying, What shall we do to these men?*
> *for that indeed a notable miracle hath*
> *been done by* ***them is manifest***
> ***to all them that dwell in Jerusalem;***
> ***and we cannot deny it.***
> *(Acts 4: 14–16)*

The elders did not like Jesus' disciples preaching in His Name, but they didn't know what to do given the miracle the disciples had performed. God will continue to bring the world to its knees where they will see His glory, look at the body of Christ and then say, "Surely the LORD, their God has done this for them and we cannot deny it."

Let's look at another recorded example of the manifested power of God in Acts, chapter 27:

> *And now I exhort you to be of good cheer:*
> *for there shall be no loss of any man's life*
> *among you, but of the ship.*
>
> *For there stood by me this night **the angel***
> ***of God**, whose I am, and whom I serve,*
> *Saying, Fear not, Paul; thou must be*
> *brought before Caesar: and, lo, **God hath***
> ***given thee all them that sail with thee**.*
>
> *Wherefore, sirs, be of good cheer: for*
> ***I believe God**, that it shall be*
> *even as it was told me.*
> *(vv. 22–25)*

In this passage, the apostle Paul has been taken prisoner and is being transported along with many other prisoners to Italy to appear before Caesar. While on the ship they run into a hurricane and the people start panicking. Many contemplate jumping overboard. In verse 24, the angel of God prophetically tells Paul his destiny: "Thou must be brought before Caesar." Knowing how the situation would turn out, Paul encourages the men not to worry because there would be no loss of lives. Paul clearly understands that it does not matter what is going on, how strong the storm is raging, or how deep the trouble is around him. The apostle knows that he is destined to appear before Caesar and that God will not allow anything to get in the way of this happening.

In verse 25, Paul basically declares glory. I assure you that at the time Paul made his proclamation, the storm was not over. The wind was still blowing and the rain was still pouring, but Paul said, "I believe God." Paul knew that he would fulfill his destiny and understood that he would survive and everyone with him would survive as well.

> *And the soldiers' counsel*
> *was to kill the prisoners,*
> *lest any of them should*
> *swim out, and escape.*
>
> *But the centurion, willing to save Paul,*
> *kept them from their purpose; and*
> *commanded that they which could*
> *swim should cast themselves*
> *first into the sea, and get to land:*
>
> *And the rest, some on boards,*
> *and some on broken pieces of the ship.*
> *And so it came to pass,*
> *that they escaped all safe to land.*
> *(Acts 27:42–44)*

In verse 42, the soldiers, using typical military logic, considered killing the prisoners to prevent their escape. However, the centurion, in his desire to save Paul let the men swim to shore. When everyone on the ship made it safely to land, as the angel of God had said they would, they realized this was an experience that could only be attributed to the manifested power of God.

Believers are certain to experience times in our lives when we shall literally behold His glory and power. We will see, hear, touch, taste, and smell the manifested promise. I believe that if Paul were anything like some of us, when he arrived to shore, he took the time to get in a quick praise. It is not recorded, but as much time as Paul spent communing with God, I believe that when he got to shore, he shouted, "Hallelujah," waved his hands, and "cut a step!"

> *And when Paul had gathered a bundle*
> *of sticks, and laid them on the fire,*
> *here came a viper*
> *out of the heat,*
> *and fastened on his hand.*
>
> *And when the barbarians saw the*
> *venomous beast hang on his hand,*
> *they said among themselves,*
> *No doubt this man is a murderer, whom,*
> *though he hath escaped the sea,*
> *yet vengeance suffereth not to live.*
>
> *And he shook off the beast into the fire,*
> *and felt no harm.*
> *(Acts 28:3–5)*

This passage describes how once on shore, Paul gathered sticks to build a fire. Just as he began to build the fire, a poisonous snake leaped out and latched onto his hand. Why am I sharing these verses with you? They send an important message. When it looks like we have the victory, we must never think that the enemy is going to give up on trying to make us doubt our destiny. Satan knows that if he can make us doubt what God has ordained for our lives, then we will never obtain the manifested promise. Paul was able to maintain his confidence in what God had declared under the worst of circumstances.

Verse 4 describes how the natives assumed that Paul must have been a murderer who deserved to die. They believed that anyone who had survived what Paul had, only to end up bitten by a poisonous snake, must have done something terribly wrong. But Paul had enough of the Word of God in his spirit, and enough trust in God that he did not start crying or acknowledge that the snake could kill him. Verse 5 notes Paul "shook off the beast into the fire, and felt no harm."

Shake It Off!

We Christians, as the body of Christ, need to understand that when the adversary does not want to let go, like Paul, we need to shake him off. As a pastor, I see too many people who let the devil turn them into "yo-yos," going up and down at the devil's whim. It is sad to watch individuals, who had a vision of the promise, lose hope because something happened to them that did not fit the vision. They do not understand that the enemy is trying to take the praise out of their hearts. If you ever find yourself in this situation, I have a message from the Holy Spirit just for you: "Don't just sit there—shake it off! Shake, shake, shake the devil off!"

> *Howbeit they looked when he should have*
> *swollen, or fallen down dead suddenly:*
> *but after they had looked a great while,*
> *and saw no harm come to him,*
> *they changed their minds,*
> *and said that he was a god.*
> *(Acts 28:6)*

In the natural, Paul should have died, but because of the supernatural power of God, he lived. The natives thought Paul was a god. What an example of God's manifested power at work! When believers remain steadfast, absolutely nothing can stop our destiny from unfolding. The blessings destined to be ours, the promises upon which we declared glory, and the things for which we trusted God will manifest. Like Paul, we shall witness *the manifested power of God!*

> *But thou hast fully known my doctrine,*
> *manner of life, purpose, faith,*
> *longsuffering, charity, patience,*
>
> *Persecutions, afflictions, which came unto*
> *me at Antioch, at Iconium, at Lystra;*
> *what persecutions I endured: but out of*
> *them all the Lord delivered me.*
> *(2 Timothy 3:10–11)*

God delivered Paul from every trial, persecution, and affliction and there is no reason the testimony of believers should not be the same as his: "But out of them all the Lord delivered me!" Why would God do this? To make our calling and election sure (2 Peter 1:10).

God declared His purpose and plan for the body of Christ before the foundation of the world and it shall come to pass. He rules the universe and controls our destiny. King David wrote in 1 Chronicles 29:12–13:

> *Both riches and honour come of thee,*
> *and thou reignest over all;*
> *and in thine hand is power and might;*
> *and in thine hand it is to make great,*
> *and to give strength unto all.*
>
> *Now therefore, our God,*
> *we thank thee, and praise*
> *thy glorious name.*

As we continue on this journey to glory, the power of God will manifest in and through our lives, ensuring that we reach our divine destination. We are called into the Kingdom (1 Thessalonians 2:12) by the gospel of Jesus Christ, to the obtaining of His glory (2 Thessalonians 2:14). He holds all power in His hand and gives us power to fulfill our destiny. Thank You LORD!

In my final chapter I want to discuss *resting* in the knowledge and hope of God's purpose and plan for your life. Those who have gotten this word into their spirits should be fully confident that the LORD shall bring it to pass. When you've done everything you know to do, trusted in Him, and stood on the Word, it is time to simply *Rest in Him.*

ELEVEN

REST IN HIM

Rest in the LORD, and wait patiently for him: fret not thyself because of him who prospereth in his way, because of the man who bringeth wicked devices to pass.
(Psalm 37:7)

As we await manifestation of the LORD's promises in our lives, it is important to keep a positive attitude. Grumbling and complaining does not make God hurry up. In fact, this negative attitude may only delay the time He has set for your blessing. In the above Scripture, we are encouraged to *rest* and be still before the Lord. The psalmist is instructing God's people to wait *patiently*, meaning, longingly or intently with expectation. We already know that God will do what He said He would do. Numbers 23:19 *NIV* assures us that God is not a man that He should lie, nor a son of man that He should change His mind. This verse goes on to ask, "Does He speak and not act? Does He promise and not fulfill?" So, in good times and in bad, when things go right and when they go wrong, the best thing for believers to do is follow the psalmist's advice: *rest in the LORD and wait patiently for Him!*

Stand Still and Watch God Move!

Have you ever been in a situation where you asked God to help you and instead of things getting better, they got worse? You knew deep in your spirit that God was going to come through for you; however, as time passed, the situation continued to head downhill. This is the perfect opportunity to be still and wait on the LORD! I am not saying that you should be in denial about the problems you face in the physical realm. However, we who *walk in the spirit* (by faith) must focus our attention on what God has declared in the spirit realm.

In the Book of Joshua, we find Joshua facing a similar situation. He was leading the children of Israel to the Promised Land, when they came to a huge obstacle— the overflowing banks of the Jordan River. In chapter 3, verse 8, God instructed Joshua to tell the priests: "When ye are come to the brink of the water of Jordan, ye shall stand *still* in Jordan." It was as if God was saying, "Stand still in your trouble or difficulty." In the natural realm, this made no sense. However, the LORD is not concerned with what you see, feel, or hear. Sometimes He just wants you to stand still and watch

Him move! When the soles of the priests' feet touched the waters of Jordan, the LORD stopped the flow of water and the children of Israel were able to pass over the Jordan River on dry land.

Fret Not

Impatience, due to a perceived lack of progress, causes some people to charge ahead of God's timing and attempt to force the unfolding of their destiny. Believers can become especially vulnerable and frustrated when it appears that people, who are not even thinking about committing to God, are moving up and prospering more quickly than they do. But Psalm 37:7b says, "Fret not thyself because of him who prospereth in his way, because of the man who bringeth wicked devices to pass." Too many times individuals become distracted by what is happening in other people's lives when they should be concentrating on God's purpose for their own lives. The LORD wants us to stay focused on fulfilling our destiny.

The temptation to compare your life with someone else's provides the adversary with an opportunity to plant a seed of doubt in your mind concerning God's plan for you. The accuser will say, "Look at you. You're faithful serving on all those committees, doing this, that, and the other. No one ever says anything about all the work you're doing. The lady who sits on the third pew looks like she really has it "going on," and she doesn't do a thing in the ministry. You are just wasting your time!"

The enemy's strategy is to get you sidetracked from your destiny. We must be careful not to fall prey to his tricks of planting seeds of jealousy, bitterness, and even resentment toward God. Focus on positioning yourself to receive from the LORD and believe that the blessing is coming to you! In the appointed time what belongs to you shall be manifested.

Vengeance Belongs to God

Cease from anger, and forsake wrath:
fret not thyself in any wise to do evil.
(Psalm 37:8)

Harboring anger and bitterness can also be a stumbling block to fulfilling one's destiny. For example, most of us personally know the pain of being deceived by a trusted friend, family member, co-worker, or even church member. When this happens, many times the first thought that comes to our minds is revenge! You may have heard that someone was spreading vicious rumors about you. Wanting to defend yourself or retaliate when someone attacks your character are natural responses. There is no need to pretend that you never experience this feeling. No one is so "saved" that they are void of negative human emotions.

I realize that God cannot help individuals who deny their true feelings; so I have learned to be honest with myself and with Him. There have been times when I have really wanted to get back at someone for what they did to me. When I feel like I am on the verge of a "flesh" moment I tell myself, *Wait a minute—It's not worth it!* I refuse to allow evil thoughts to consume my soul and distract me from fulfilling my God-given purpose. The LORD will fight my battles because vengeance belongs to Him (2 Chronicles 20:15, Romans 12:19, and Hebrews 10:30).

> *For evildoers shall be cut off:*
> *but those that wait upon the LORD,*
> ***they shall inherit the earth.***
> *(Psalm 37:9)*

Scripture proclaims, "Evildoers shall be cut off," but for some reason there are numerous church people who feel the need to "call down fire from heaven" on anyone they believe has done something wrong to them. "You have messed with the wrong one this time," they shout. My advice to these believers is to study the Word. It clearly tells us not to worry or dwell on the actions of evil doers because they shall be cut off.

Christians in pursuit of their destiny do not have time to waste thinking about the ill-gotten gains of the unrighteous. We are the ones who are destined to take possession of the earth. Psalm 37:9 does not say that it might, maybe, or there's a good chance it could happen. It says that those who wait upon the LORD shall inherit the earth and that includes everything in it! God's promises are filled with prosperity (kindness, joyfulness, peace, safety, and wealth). The manifested blessing makes us rich and we shall have no sorrow with it (Proverbs 10:22).

It is particularly important for young believers to learn how to be patient and rest in the Lord. Let's be honest: the church loses some of its effectiveness in reaching young people when they see drug dealers in fine clothes and fancy cars while believers are in hand-me-downs and rusty putt-putts. Many of our youth look at these drug dealers and say, "Man they've got it going on." To counteract these negative influences, the church needs to encourage young people to pursue the blessings of God and show them how prosperity is being poured out on the body of Christ.

Let the World See You Blessed

The world needs to see our blessings. Many believers have been taught to keep their prosperity hidden. However, in the times of the Old Testament, gifts of jewelry and other expensive items were often given to demonstrate a person's level of prosperity as well as prove the sincerity of one's intentions. In Genesis, chapter 24, Abraham gave Eliezer, his servant, specific instructions on finding a wife for Isaac, his son of promise. Let's read verses 29–31:

> *And Rebekah had a brother,*
> *and his name was Laban:*
> *and Laban ran out unto*
> *the man [Eliezer], unto the well.*

> *And it came to pass,*
> *when he saw the earring and bracelets*
> *upon his sister's hands,*
> *and when he heard the words*
> *of Rebekah his sister, saying,*
> *Thus spake the man unto me;*
> *that he came unto the man; and,*
> *behold, he stood by the camels at the well.*
>
> *And he said, Come in, thou blessed of the*
> *LORD; wherefore standest thou without?*
> *for I have prepared the house,*
> *and room for the camels.*

Laban, Rebekah's brother, *saw* the jewelry Abraham's servant had given her and heard the report of his master's great wealth. In verse 31, Laban called Eliezer "blessed of the LORD." Rebekah's family was both pleased and impressed with what they *saw* and heard.

Even today, we must show the world that we are blessed! As the commanded blessings overtake us, we will have wealth and riches, be in health and wholeness, and our families shall live in peace and prosperity.

The Law of First Mention

People who are *destined for glory* are destined for wealth. Let me illustrate what I mean with the following assignment. Look for the first occurrence of the word *glory* in the Bible. An important hermeneutic method of study I use is the Law of First Mention.

When studying Scripture, if one can understand a term when it is first mentioned in the Bible, then it may help with relating to other references. You will find *glory* first mentioned in Genesis 31:1 which reads:

> *And he heard the words of Laban's sons,*
> *saying, Jacob hath taken away all that*
> *was our father's; and of that which was*
> *our father's hath he gotten all this* **glory***.*

The *Amplified Bible* reads:

> *Jacob heard Laban's sons complaining,*
> *Jacob has taken away all that*
> *was our Father's; he has acquired all*
> *this wealth and honor from*
> *what belonged to our father.*

Isaac and Rebekah had sent Jacob away from Canaan to flee the wrath of Esau, his brother (Esau's anger was kindled when Jacob used trickery to gain possession of Esau's birthright). During Jacob's sojourn to his mother's homeland he became very wealthy. The above Scripture states that he had gotten *glory*. In other words, Jacob was abounding with honor, esteem, majesty, abundance, and wealth. Jacob's destiny is our destiny. According to Galatians 3:29, if we belong to Christ we are Abraham's seed; and, therefore, heirs according to the promise. As the seed of Abraham, Jacob was destined to be blessed and show forth God's *glory*. The *glory* that Jacob received, as the seed of Abraham, is the same *glory* the LORD promised He would give to us.

Nothing Missing, Nothing Broken

But the meek shall inherit the earth;
and shall delight themselves
in the abundance of peace.
(Psalm 37:11)

The Word of God tells us, "The meek shall inherit the earth; and shall delight themselves in the abundance of peace." Unfortunately, many in the body of Christ do not understand what the Bible means when it describes someone as meek. These people tend to think that meekness means being passive, having few possessions, and being satisfied with one's low socioeconomic position in life. However, *meek* in this Scripture passage refers to having a mindset of humility and lowliness in thought of one's self in relationship to God. When we see ourselves as clay and our Creator as the Potter, we will be totally dependent upon Him. Operating on this level of meekness and embracing God's plan for our lives will position us to receive our inheritance (glory/wealth) and eat the good of the land.

Believers who humbly submit to God's divine purpose shall possess the earth and the fullness thereof (Psalm 24:1). There shall be no lack in any area of our lives. *Peace* in Psalm 37:11 comes from the Hebrew word *shalom*, which means safety, completeness, soundness, health, and prosperity. In the abundance of peace we have wholeness—*nothing is missing or broken.*

Blessings that were prepared for us from the very beginning are waiting to be claimed (Proverbs 13:22b). The *Amplified Bible* makes this verse very clear. It reads:

179

> "...And the wealth of the sinner
> [finds its way eventually]
> into the hands of the righteous,
> for whom it was laid up."

The adversary tried to take our wealth away, but Jesus came to restore it to the rightful owners. John 10:10 tells us that the thief came to steal, kill, and destroy, but Jesus came to give us an abundance of life. Our Lord and Savior turns our situation around and destroys the works of the devil (1 John 3:8)! The Bible says, "For since the beginning of the world men have not heard, nor perceived by the ear, neither hath the eye seen, O God, beside thee, what he hath prepared for him that waiteth for him" (Isaiah 64:4). Those who want to delight in the abundance of peace must be willing to wait with a quiet but confident spirit before the LORD. Wait on the LORD: ...wait, I say, on the LORD! (Psalm 27:14)

It's Time for Manifestation

As stated in the previous chapter, when something manifests it has become evident or apparent to the senses, particularly that of sight. The LORD is putting visible blessings in our hands that the world can plainly and clearly see. We are allowed to enjoy and partake of the manifested promises; however, we must remember they are for His *glory*. The LORD wants to get a blessing through us, so that we can reflect His glory back to Him.

Let me tell you something about me that you might not know. I am a preacher who believes *everything* in the Bible is true. I have no problem expecting results when I pray and rebuke disease out of someone's body or curse the spirit of confusion in the Name of Jesus Christ. Similarly, when I speak of God's promises concerning wealth being released to the body of Christ, I expect tangible results. God is not slack concerning His promise (2 Peter 3:9). Delivery of the blessings that were spoken for His children before the foundation of the world is guaranteed (Ephesians 1:3–4).

As I look back over my life, no one can tell me what God won't do. Though I was blessed with wonderful and loving parents, they were not wealthy to the extent where they could give me a truckload of money when I became an adult. When I left home to live on my own, the only thing my parents gave me was their blessing. They said, "May the LORD bless you! Goodbye!" Though they said goodbye, God didn't say goodbye. I am a witness that God will bless you abundantly, regardless of which side of the tracks you come from. If you have the proper attitude to receive His purpose and plan for your life, it shall be done.

Live in Expectation

Believers should be excited and optimistic about their destiny. If someone does not expect the fulfillment of God's purpose and plan for his or her life, it will never happen. However, when a person stands on the Word of God and proclaims, "I expect to be blessed because the Bible says I'm blessed"—it will happen for that individual!

Don't be disturbed if you are barely making it right now. Lift up your head, get your praise on and say, "This is a temporary situation and soon I will be on my way!" Be confident that you will do well because it is God's plan that you prosper in every aspect of your life.

Many in the world, and even some from the traditional church, would have us believe that it is not God's will for Christians to prosper. Years ago Christians who lived in prosperity or even desired to do so were considered carnal-minded. Yet, even as a teenager, I knew that God intended for believers to prosper, and I have always had the desire to be successful. When I was fifteen years old, I got my first job selling shoes at U.S. Shoe Corporation, where I made $2.00 an hour. This was during the time of the "Big Red Machine." The Cincinnati Reds baseball team had many stars who would frequently shop at the store including Pete Rose, Joe Morgan, Ken Griffey, Sr., Tony Perez, and Johnny Bench.

Even through I dreamed of playing professional baseball, deep inside I knew there was no chance of that ever happening. As I looked at some of those wealthy athletes I thought, *Now God, as a saved young man, how do I get rich!*

As the have years passed, my life has become a testimony that if God's children obey and serve Him, we shall prosper and live in abundance. Anyone who has seen the building where I began serving as pastor in 1990 knows that my ministry started from very humble beginnings. Though I was often ridiculed and the brunt of cruel jokes, I was determined to remain faithful and steadfast. I let the LORD know that I trusted His will for my life and that I would do whatever He wanted. My goal then and now is to fulfill His purpose and plan, allowing His glory to be revealed through me.

If you, too, are trusting God to manifest His Word in your life, do not be surprised when people laugh at you. Just remember, we serve a God who uses the foolish things of the world to confound the wise (1 Corinthians 1:27). As you stand firm in His Word, before you know it, God will begin putting dreams and visions in your spirit. He will give you a glimpse of the glorious future He has planned for you. God wants you to be encouraged and motivated as you strive to give Him glory and honor.

Our current church sanctuary seats over 500 people and we now have over 1,800 members. When I first embarked on building our church, the architect provided an artist's rendering of the completed structure. Yet, the vision God gave me still seemed very far away. I now realize that in the natural realm, though it appeared we were far from the vision, in the spirit we were on the brink of manifestation. Today, we have an artist's rendering *and* model of our future 5000-seat worship facility and family life center. Once again, the LORD has placed a vision in my spirit that I know He shall surely bring to pass!

The Wait Is Over!

Recently, I tossed and turned all night, then I asked the Lord, "What is it?" He responded, "I want you to curse every hindrance of the power of the enemy that is stopping the blessings from getting into the hands of My people." I immediately began to rebuke the devil in the Name of Jesus Christ. The LORD told me that this is the season for manifestation of His blessings and to declare that *the wait is over!* It's time for the body of Christ to take possession of the promise!

The LORD also told me, "There are people whose blessings are being held up by the adversary. Even though they have carefully positioned themselves to receive from Me, there is a spiritual battle being fought against them." Then He said, "Hilton, I give you the authority to rebuke the devourer and release their blessings."

On the following Sunday, I stood in the pulpit and by the power in the Name of Jesus Christ, I rebuked every spirit of the adversary that was hindering the progress and prosperity of God's people! By the authority of Jesus' Name, I released blessings! And because God said it, I declared that *the wait was over* and that people would receive abundantly. Hallelujah!

Dwell Therein Forever

This word to the body of Christ is as important as any message I have ever taught. The Bible says, "The righteous shall inherit the land and dwell therein forever" (Psalm 37:29). The LORD has anointed me to tell His people that we shall live in wealth because of the things we must accomplish for His Kingdom.

This anointing on my life was confirmed during a conference hosted by Bishop Brian Keith Williams, senior pastor of All Nations Church in Columbus, OH. On the night when I was the featured speaker, Bishop Williams and Bishop George Rueben Scott of Christ Worldwide Church in Dayton, Ohio began to prophesy. They told me that God had anointed me to destroy the spirits of debt, lack, and insufficiency. They stated that I was assigned to release wealth, prosperity, and abundance to the body of Christ. They began to tell me about all the places I would go because of my specific assignment to get wealth into the hands of God's people for His work.

I take this God-given assignment very seriously and declare by the anointing of Jesus Christ (which removes burdens and destroys yokes), that anything the enemy has devised to hinder our prosperity shall be cast down. It's time for every believer to prosper and be blessed! This is the will of God for us. I prophesy to all who receive this word that you shall have more than enough money to support God's Kingdom and bless others. Your cup will run over with blessings from the LORD!

Enlarge My Territory

And Jabez called on the God of Israel, saying,
Oh that thou wouldest bless me indeed,
and enlarge my coast, and that thine hand
might be with me, and that thou wouldest

keep me from evil, that it may not grieve me!
And God granted him that which he requested.
(1 Chronicles 4:10)

Some Christians fear overflowing blessings, but Scripture shows us when we have the right motive, there is nothing wrong with asking God to enlarge our territory. The prayer of Jabez is a good example. According to Scripture, Jabez was more honorable than his brothers, despite his name, which means, distress, sorrows, and giver of pain. Could it be that because of the spirit associated with his name, he learned early in life to seek the LORD? In the *Living Bible,* verse 9 says, "He was more distinguished than his brothers" and then verse 10 goes on to say, "He was *the one* who prayed to the God of Israel." It is often the furnace of afflictions and wilderness experiences that propel us to intensify our prayer life, and thus grow spiritually mature.

When Jabez asked the LORD, "Bless me indeed," he was saying, in essence, "Empower me to prosper, equip me to succeed, and position me to live in abundance." Jabez also asked the LORD to enlarge his territory; that is, to increase his boundaries and make him profitable and wealthy. Why did Jabez ask this of God? To intensify the vision within him and maximize his potential whereby *God's glory* would be revealed. Jabez also petitioned God, "That Thine hand might be with me." This could be interpreted as requesting divine help, intervention, and aid from God. In Scripture, the hand of God usually denotes His power, His control, and His authority. Christians who humbly submit to God should never hold back from requesting the presence of His hand. Lastly, Jabez asked that evil and harm be kept from him. It is vital that we ask God to keep all hurt, harm, and danger away from us so that we will not become sorrowful and distracted from our destiny.

God granted Jabez's request, and He will grant ours too. Do you want your destiny? As for me, I've got to have it! I have come to the point where I will not settle for anything less than the manifested power and glory of *God* operating in my life. I want God to *bless me indeed* and *enlarge my territory!*

An Expected End

> *For I know the thoughts that I think*
> *toward you, saith the LORD,*
> *thoughts of peace, and not of evil,*
> *to give you an expected end.*
> *(Jeremiah 29:11)*

God has a set time when He will visit us and perform His good Word of promises toward us. He wants the best for His children. The thoughts that the LORD has toward us are those of peace, love, and prosperity. And, because of Jesus Christ, we possess them all.

When you find yourself trying to design your own life, think about the fact that God created a divine plan especially for you. You are a designer's original; His purpose for your life is greater than anything you ever imagined. Receive it now and obtain every good and perfect gift (James 1:17).

God's Word Never Fails

*Blessed be the LORD, that hath given rest
unto his people Israel, according to all that
he promised: there hath not failed one word
of all his good promise, which he promised
by the hand of Moses his servant.*
(1 Kings 8:56)

Even with the many issues and the cares of life, you can rest in the LORD because His Word never fails! It is important for the believers to know that in the Word of God they will find a promise to address any problem. In this verse from the Book of 1 Kings, we see that God remained faithful to every jot and tittle of His Word (Matthew 5:18). The LORD spoke these promises, first to Abram (later renamed Abraham) then reiterated them to his seed, Isaac and Jacob. Hundreds of years later, God brought them to pass by the hand of Moses.

When you place yourself in agreement with God's Word, as issues and cares of life arise—and they will—you can rest peacefully knowing He has divinely arranged things. You are *Destined for Glory!* The LORD's magnificence shall operate mightily in your life and the world will know that He is a God who is faithful to His Word. *Rest in Him* and meditate on His promises. May the peace of the LORD that passes all understanding be yours, as you embrace His purpose and plan for your life.

A Prayer of Destiny

Heavenly Father we come to You in the precious Name of Our Lord and Savior Jesus Christ. You are an awesome God and Sovereign Creator. We thank You for selecting us to have Your *glory* revealed through our lives. We humbly submit ourselves to Your preordained purpose and plan. Please let Your Spirit lift, encourage, and strengthen us, as we learn to endure and overcome any obstacle on our path to destiny.

We thank You for Your Word which lets us know that we can call those things that be not, as though they were. Therefore we declare, "What will be already is." We thank You that Your Kingdom has come and Thy perfect will is done in earth, as it is in Heaven.

LORD, *bless us indeed!* Empower us to prosper, equip us to succeed, and position us to live in abundance. *Enlarge our coasts*, so that our boundaries and territories are increased, causing us to profit and live in wealthy places. LORD, intensify our vision and maximize our potential to show forth Your *glory*. We pray that *Your hand be upon us,* to guide and direct us. We ask You to *keep all evil from us* so that no hurt, harm, or danger will distract us from reaching our destiny.

The God-ordained purpose for our lives shall be fulfilled. LORD, we thank You for Your peace and for the spirit of oneness that binds our hearts and minds together. We give You all glory, honor, and praise. We call these done in the Name of Jesus Christ. Amen.

ANOTHER *Life–Changing* BOOK

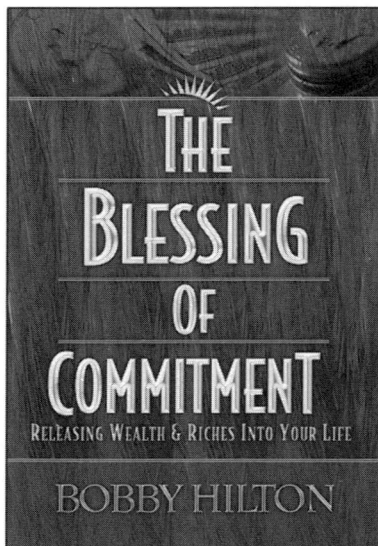

If you're expecting God to do great things through you and for you, this book is a must-read.
—Dr. Creflo A. Dollar

Bishop Bobby Hilton, a voice to our generation has provided us a pattern, a process, and an opportunity to commit to eternal values and see incredible results. This book will create a pathway to genuine blessing.
—Dr. Mark J. Chironna

Bishop Hilton has effectively isolated the time-tested principle that guarantee success and equip readers with the tools to experience God's best in life.
—Dr. Myles Munroe

Bishop Bobby Hilton provides sound Biblical principles and practical applications at a time when many teachings on prosperity resemble secular, get-rich-quick schemes. Bishop Hilton shows readers the true pathway to obtaining the wealth and riches God has declared for the Kingdom.

The Blessing of Commitment
Bishop Bobby Hilton
ISBN:1-930766-25-4
Trade:172 pages
Price: $12.99

COVENANT PARTNERSHIP

We have a special gift for you for becoming a Covenant Partner!

Would you prayerfully consider becoming a PARTNER? If the Lord is touching your heart, please have enough faith and courage to say **Yes** to His leading. When you join in partnership with us, we will send you our complimentary New Covenant Partner Packet. You will receive a FREE audio tape, certificate, and a discount card, which saves you 10% off purchases of products from the ministry.

Become a Covenant Partner with us **TODAY** and receive your free 4-tape series of *THE POWER OF UNITY!*

In this series, Bishop Bobby Hilton teaches us that unity can overcome all barriers, including denominational and racial. Our love for each other, combined with prayer and praise, can help us reach unlimited heights for the Kingdom.

This *life changing* 4-tape audio series is yours to enjoy, free and postage paid, for a ministry gift of only $25. Get ready to feel The Power of Unity as Bishop Bobby Hilton shows believers how to break through the wall of division and tap into the source of real power!

Covenant Partnership Form

To place an order by phone, please call:
(513) 851-WORD(9673)
If calling outside of Cincinnati, Ohio, please use: 1-877-851-WORD(9673)
Tuesday - Friday 9:00 AM - 5:30 PM (EST)
Please allow 1-3 weeks for delivery.

Make checks or money orders payable to: Bishop Bobby Hilton Ministries
To fax your order: (513) 742-3458

I would like to be a Covenant Partner with Bishop Bobby Hilton Ministries, Inc. with a monthly gift of:

____$10 ____$25 ____$50 ____$100 ____$Other (for at least a $25 ministry gift, you will receive your free postage-paid 4-tape series - Power of Unity)

Please print clearly.

Name_____

Address_____

City_____State_____

Zip_____ Phone (____)_____

METHOD OF PAYMENT
(____) Check or Money Order
(____) Bank Card (check one)
☐AMEX ☐MC ☐VISA ☐DISC   Exp. Date_____
Card#_____
Signature_____

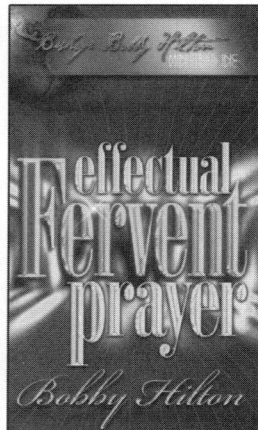